ISSUES IN
ARTIFICIAL INTELLIGENCE

Edited by
Tangaza University

ISSUES IN ARTIFICIAL INTELLIGENCE:
A PHILOSOPHICAL INTERROGATION
Conference Proceedings III from Tangaza University

Preface by Munguci D. Etriga, AJ &
Introduction by Theophilus Chando

Domuni-Press

2025

THIS BOOK IS PUBLISHED
BY DOMUNI-PRESS
RESEARCH COLLECTION

Philosophy

ISSN: 2607-9321
ISBN: 978-2-36648-231-7
© DOMUNI-PRESS, July 2025

The intellectual property code prohibits copies or reproductions intended for collective use. Representation or reproduction in whole or in part by any means whatsoever, without the consent of the author or his successors, is unlawful and constitutes an infringement of copyright under articles L.335-2 and following of the Intellectual Property Code.

TANGAZA UNIVERSITY
P.O. Box 15055– 00509 Langata Nairobi
Tell: 020-2379048/0722-204724

INSTITUTE OF PHILOSOPHY

Tangaza University is a Catholic institution of higher learning. Started in 1986 in Nairobi -Kenya, the University hosts three schools: School of Theology (SOT), School of Education (SOE); and School of Arts and Social Sciences (SASS). The SOT is the biggest Catholic Philosophical and Theological centre in Africa, with students and lecturers from over 40 countries and approximately 100 Religious and or Missionary Institutes/Orders. The University is distinguished for academic excellence, service orientation and a commitment to social transformation under the motto: *Teaching Minds, Touching Hearts, and Transforming Lives.* Tangaza Institute of Philosophy, which is one of the four institutes in the SOT, holds an annual International Philosophy Conference on the feast day of St. Thomas Aquinas – the Institute's patron. The year 2024's conference had for its theme: *Issues in Artificial Intelligence: A Philosophical Interrogation.*

Preface and Acknowledgments

The current and drastic advances in Artificial Intelligence (AI) present humanity with one of the most profound philosophical challenges. As machines increasingly become human synonyms capable of multitasking what primordially were preserves for the domain of human intellect, we are compelled to raise certain fundamental philosophical questions about intelligence, consciousness, will and the nature of human person itself.

Tangaza University (TU), through the Institute of Philosophy (IOP), has the unique privilege of hosting an annual international philosophy day marked by a symposium. It serves as a forum for philosophers, technologists and scholars of various fields to explore and reflect on pertinent and emergent philosophical issues of human life and society. This is not just as a matter of academic calisthenics. It has practical and existential import for understanding of ourselves and societies in order to advance the quality of our existence now and tomorrow.

The 2024's international philosophy symposium was thus dedicated to interrogating issues in AI. I've been fortunate to chair the Symposium Steering Committee (SSC) that organizes the event. Accordingly, I was privileged to receive lots of articles from various eminent researchers who donated some of their valuable time towards this course. This book, christened, *Philosophy Conference Proceedings III*, is the upsot.

The book is divided into four parts. Part one, which has two chapters, establishes the philosophical antecedents of AI. Chapter one, *The Philosophical Roots of the Generative Pre-trained Transformer Chatterbots*, attempts to demonstrate the link between logic, Computer language programs, and AI. Chapter two, *The Phenomenology of Human Subjectivity in the Hi-Tech rationality*, delves into the phenomenon of AI. It underscores that the presence of advanced technologies in the lived-experience of the modern subject is an issue that challenges the being of the human person that must be interrogated for achieving her meaningful existence.

Part two of the book, also consisting of two chapters: three and four, addresses AI and the Epistemic questions, by discussing the epistemic structure and its relation to AI. Chapter III, *A Critical Evaluation of Lonergan's Concept of Human Understanding and AI*, analyses the human intelligence as the foundation of AI. In Chapter IV, *The Abyss Between Human and Artificial Intelligence*, the book attempts a critical examination of the relationship between AI and its maker – the human person. It seeks to demonstrate that between Human Intelligence (HI) and AI, there is an unbridgeable gap, though the two are, somewhat, interdependent. On the one hand, while AI is dependent on HI for existence and functionality, on the other hand, the latter (HI) is dependent on the former (AI) for enhancement of its efficiency.

Part three of the book, consisting of three chapters, treats some moral questions raised by AI. Chapter V, *AI and Free Will: Critical Perspectives Based on Saint Thomas Aquinas's Concept of* Liberum Arbitrium, is dedicated to the analysis of the moral faculty of will and its implications for decision-making actions performed by AI. It analyses the automaton theory based on a deterministic framework that challenges the possibility of free will, while taking into consideration the process of deliberation, intentionality and the ultimate end of the free act. In Chapter VI, *An Evaluation of the Philosophy of AI Through the Kantian Lenses of Free-Will*, the book interrogates AI through the eyes of the Philosopher, Immanual Kant, trying to establish the moral implications of AI for the notions of freedom and autonomy. Chapter VII, *Human-Artificial Intelligence Relationship: A Moral Inquiry from Heideggerian Perspective*, exorts a thoughtful and reflective approach to the development and implementation of AI technologies, grounded on an awareness of their profound impact on the moral fabric of human existence.

Part four of the book, concludes the philosophical interrogations of AI. It examines the AI and anthropological question in Chapter VIII, through *Artificial Intelligence and the Question of Artificial Person: Possibility or Hot Air?* The chapter directly brings to the fore the underlying tension evident throughout the Chapters of the book, that is, the question as to whether AI and the Human Person are or can be identical. The Chapter ultimately concludes that the concept 'artificial-intelligence' belies any prospects for possibility of person: human or artificial.

PREFACE AND ACKNOWLEDGMENTS

Finally, on behalf of the SSC, I'm grateful to all the contributors and other players who made the 2024 symposium event a success, right from its inception to publication to which this book is a testimony. The SSC is particularly cognizant of the offices of DVC Academics, Research and Students' Life (DVCAR&SL), and Director Institutional Advancement (DIA) for rendering the needed support towards this realization. And to you the reader of the book, may you find something of value and inspiration!

Thanks.

Munguci D. Etriga, AJ
Nairobi, 2023

Introduction

Theophilus Chando, Theophilus Chando holds a PhD in Philosophy, with a focus on Political Philosophy. He wrote the Introduction and is the Chief Editor. He teaches at The Technical University of Kenya where he is, also, the Academic Team Leader (ATL), of the Department of Philosophy and Liberal Studies. Besides teaching in many other institutions, he, also, is a consultant Lecturer at the Military University, the National Defence University of Kenya, Lanet, Nakuru. His research interests include, Political Theory, Critical and Creative Thinking, Logic, Epistemology, Security Studies, and Foreign Policy Analysis.

Artificial Intelligence, popularly known by its abbreviation, AI, is a milestone in the trajectory of human intellectual dynamism. The birth of computers was certainly a revolutionary event for humanity. It is a revolution that has had a profound impact on the course of human history. AI is a product of the computer era, arising out of the different aspects of computer software engineering that attempt to manipulate information. The most robust beneficiary of AI is the Information and Communications Technology, ICT. Today, collecting, coding, analysing, and using information is way easier than was the case about half a century ago. With AI, further development has been witnessed where information can be manipulated to create g43reater and more complex extrapolations of greater impacts extremely shorter period.

The history of AI is rather imprecise. While formal records place the origins of AI around 1956 with the coinage of the word by John McCarthy, there are claims that AI began with the works of American McCulloch and Walter Pitts' presentation of their *model of artificial neurons*, in 1943, owing to the development of cybernetics.[1] Yet, residual manifestations of this technology are traced even further back in the history of philosophy in philosophical figures like Blaise Pascal and G. W. Leibniz. Concerned to help his father with his financial accounting tasks, Blaise Pascal designed what came to be known as the Pascaline, a mechanical calculator, which goes in history as one of the

---

[1] David Vernon and Demort Furlog. "Philosophical Fouondations of AI." *DBLP*. Conference Paper. DIO 10.1007/978-3-540-77296-5_6. January, 2006.

earliest attempts to invent a computer. G. W. Leibniz would, later in the 19th Century, work out an improved version of the machine.[2] In the 20th century, much of this work would occupy the minds of thinkers, especially, those who had, by now, taken a specialisation in the science of computing. In 1950, for instance, "...the British mathematician Alan Turing published an article entitled 'Computing machinery and intelligence,' ...where he asked the question: Can machines think?"[3] Turing questioned the idea that intelligence can only be natural, intimating that mind can exist in a body that is not, necessarily, human. This was the basis of the experiments which intended to determine whether machines would produce intelligence similar, or analogous to human intelligence. This Artificial Intelligence is, fundamentally, dependent on computer coding systems for its functionality. It's the capital is a series of computer digital codes which have the capacity to interpreter and express the implications of the interpretations. *Issues in Artificial Intelligence: A Philosophical Interrogation*, is an attempt to interrogate the implications of the development of the technology of Artificial Intelligence for the human agency. The various Chapters in this book present forceful arguments about the position of the human intellect vis à vis Artificial Intelligence, maintaining that AI is a product and simulation of the human cognitive capacities. Humans are cognitive symbolic, i.e., human cognitive activities are expressed in symbols-the characteristic that they have objectified in artefacts of different descriptions and purposes. AI is the most powerful demonstration of this. AI operates on quasi-human capacity to manipulate its own symbolic systems producing more symbolic patterns, building more abstract presentations.

In the AI debate, there are two theories of the role of cognition at the centre: 1) Cognitivism, which maintains that "...the role of cognition is to abstract objective structure and meaning through perception and reasoning,"[4] and inactivism, which maintains that "...the purpose of cognition is to uncover unspecified regularity and order that can then be constructed as meaningful because they facilitate the continuing

---

[2] Britanica.com/technology/Pascaline. 23/10/2024.

[3] Vernon and Frulog. "Philosophical Foundations of AI. P. 56

[4] Verno and Furlong. "Philosophical Foundations of AI," P. 8

operation and development of the cognitive system."⁵ The human mind operates in both two ways. It gets insight into the structure of reality through sensory perception and reasoning, as well as recognising patterns in objects, which it uses to construct its own categories of operation and extrapolations of meaning. This is the principle that the human agent has fitted into the computer system, which goes by the name of AI. Thus, machines can perform what in ordinary circumstances, only humans are expected to perform. This is fascinating, for with automation, computers can produce an output that humans would find impossible to produce. Yet a fundamental question still begs for an answer, and this is about the very notion of intelligence, itself. Can machines rightly be called intelligent? Can intelligence be constructed by work of art? There is a measure of controversy in this matter. One side of the argument defines intelligence as an essential characteristic of humans and cannot be attributed to objects other than humans, not even to other sentient animals than human. For that reason, it would be a case of gross misnaming, to apply the notion to works of art. The other side of the argument avers that anything that exhibits behaviour similar or analogous to that of intelligent beings can, legitimately, be designated intelligent. The convention conception of AI is any human constructed tools/artifacts (hence artificial) and systems that operate in a fashion that simulates and replicates the human intellect (hence intelligence).

Issues in Artificial Intelligence: A Philosophical Interrogation, wades into this debate from a philosophical focal point which can be characterised as an interrogation of the phenomenon of *understanding*. This is the point of departure between what is called Artificial Intelligence and Human Intelligence. The Chapters in the book centre around understanding as the hallmark of intelligence and argue that whereas machines can perform extremely complicated actions, some of which outstrip human capacity in great measure, machines do not *understand* their performances. For this reason, they cannot be, strictly, termed intelligent. Intelligence involves a lot more than what can be attributed to machines. A few examples may illustrate our point, here.

Humans evaluate actions in terms of right and wrong, good or bad, just or unjust, pleasant or unpleasant, joyful or sad. This implies a

---
⁵ Vernon and Furlog. Philosophical Foundaitons of AI," P. 8.

moral consciousness based on standards of morality, and an insight into the appropriateness or otherwise of these actions based on these standards. In so far as AI can make decisions which have moral implications, to evaluate these actions based on self-generated standards of action is an ethical capability that does not belong to the action categories of AI. It is not possible for AI operations to understand the emotional content that influences actions and judge them according to the emotional influences. When AI actions present ethical dilemmas, it is impossible to accuse AI of being ethically insensitive to those affected by its actions, or even to hold AI morally and ethically responsible for the outcome of its actions. Yet this kind of responsibility is the hallmark of human intelligence, and of intelligence as such. In a further extrapolation, it would be impossible, on this very basis, to try and formulate a code of legal responsibilities for AI according to which some legal procedures may be administered in case of a misconduct. It would be ridiculous, for instance, to subject AI to criminal procedure, should it perform acts which are injurious to us. If a self-driving car hits and kills a pedestrian, for instance, it would be impossible to seek redress in a court of law, for this kind of injury. This is because, AI does not understand the notion of legal and or moral/ethical responsibility. Lacking a will, they cannot be regarded as moral persons, and therefore, members of the moral community.

Humans, Aristotle had revealed, are teleological creatures. They act with an end in view. They have originary agency in terms of setting the purpose for their action and the means to achieve it. As one endeavours to achieve a goal, he/she may discover in the process, that the purpose is not entirely beneficial, or that the purpose may, contrary to his/her earlier estimation, be unworthy of his/her pursuit, or that the means for achieving this goal is not appropriate. He/she may even discover that both the means and the purpose are not worth pursuing, after all. In this case, a decision to alter either purpose or the means, or to abandon the entire endeavour, altogether shall have to be made. This decision is pedestalled upon the understanding of the moral value of the purpose and the means. Paramount doubt still exists, today, about AI's ability to conduct itself on such principles.

The foregoing consideration leads us, yet to another closely related matter, but which must be treated separately because of the epistemic implications I extrapolate from it. The main reason for which

INTRODUCTION

AI has been developed is to make human labour efficient. Humans, as we have seen, are teleological: they design work according to purpose. Their labour is not without an objective, and when the objective is not met, they get frustrated and either begin afresh using different methods, or they redesign the entire work enterprise, altogether. They may seek ideas from fellow humans as they work on their new strategy for achieving their purpose, which may take a long time, depending on circumstances, until they get it right. Now, in the case where a team of AI machines (read: robots) are detailed to work on improving the quality of legal services for the residents of Migori County, for instance, is it conceivable that when in doubt about how to prescribe just punishment for offenders found relieving themselves by the County Market fence at dusk, the robots may ask to benchmark with Mauritanian robots who have dealt with a similar situation, successfully? Knowledge builds upon its own foundations. Can AI construct foundational knowledge from which it may build, forming traditions, which result into culture? Again, a test for the phenomenon of understanding in AI stands strong, here.

Another issue which has characterised both academic and non-academic discourse about AI concerns the employment of AI in analysis and predicting human behaviour. It is an issue that has quite some serious implications on human dignity and human security that this calls for. Philosophically, humans are kingdoms of ends, Immanuel Kant instructs us. This implies that a treatment that devalues their status as beings of reason and creators of circumstances and destinies is inappropriate for them. Subjecting them to such analytical procedures would make of humans, mere objects rather than subjects of moral dignity, worthy of respect. Apart from the issues of biasness and intrusion into individual privacy of persons which can also be considered alongside the foregoing consideration, subjecting humans to a behavioural analysis process carried out by AI is tantamount to treating them as means to ends, rather than as ends in themselves. The Chapters of this book looking at the Kantian ethical tradition against AI are emphatic that humans, as rational beings, must maintain the ethical hegemony they have over other material creatures, including artificial creatures crafted by men and women, like AI.

From a rather generic viewpoint, intelligence is the ability to acquire information, process it, and employ it for some purpose. There are, philosophically speaking, two main ways of acquiring information: the immanently generated process, and testimony. Our concern, here, is with the first, but a brief explanation of the second is necessary. In knowledge via testimony, our primary source is the witness, who gives us the information, and on his/her authority, we accept the truth of the information. Accepting, i.e., believing the testimony of the witness as true account of the information has two implications. The recipient of the testimony believes the testimony because he/she believes that: 1) the witness is knowledgeable. A person who is not knowledgeable keeps giving information that he/she is not sure of, and contrary evidence keeps proving that the witness' information was incorrect, this is a conclusive ground for not believing anything this witness says, and for keeping oneself on one's guard in regard to this witness, always. 2) the witness is honest. A dishonest person, whether knowledgeable, is a dangerous person to believe. He/she may have the complete and correct version of the information, but he/she may decide to lie about it, for whatever reason he/she thinks good. So, the second source of knowledge has these two elements regarding its source, that must be taken care of first, before it can be endorsed.

Immanently generated knowledge involves direct contact between the knower and the known, without the mediation of a witness. Its origin is direct experience of objects of knowledge through the senses of sight, smell, hearing, taste, and touch. As the knower goes through the sensory experience, he/she generates the concepts through what we call simple apprehension, which he/she uses to make judgments expressed in propositions. With propositions such formed, the basis of argumentation and inference is established, and the knowledge which was just in potency has been made actual and can be transferred from one person to another. This, in summary, is Bernard Frederick Joseph Lonergan's cognitional theory, which we endorse. The question to explore in this matter, now, is: can artificial intelligence acquire immanently generated knowledge, in the manner outlined above? If this were to happen, then we would be talking about human, rather than artificial intelligence. The immanently generated knowledge is possible only for organic sentient beings, which artificial intelligence devices are not. The implication of this argument is that devices of artificial intelligence cannot be considered intelligent beings, in the

INTRODUCTION

strict sense of the term. The use of the term "intelligence" in regard to them must only be made derivatively and analogously.

The excitement that has characterized the world of information technology about the so-called artificial intelligence must be re-evaluated, based on sound philosophical (epistemological) principles, if we are to maintain the right focus of development, as humans. As the first two chapters of this book demonstrate, artificial intelligence is fundamentally dependent on philosophical thought, and its development stands in need of constant philosophical evaluation. There is, as we have attempted to demonstrate, a wide abyss between human and artificial intelligence, as one is organic, and the other is mechanical. To compare these two types of intelligence is to be guilty of a certain species of category mistake, attempting to apply what essentially belongs to humans, to machines. This can, (and has in fact caused) a lot of confusion among humans, as some humans have treated machines as though they were human persons. Attempting to engage robots in reproductive activities is a demonstration of deeply rooted cultural degradation, which requires urgent philosophical reconstruction. Philosophy needs to, urgently, reclaim its position as the corrective science and provide its royal services in leading humanity into the direction of the life of reason, rather than that of a life directed by emotions. Short of this, a self-constructed disaster will inflict humanity, with terribly devastating consequences; for a society whose reason has been taken hostage by emotions must wait for a catastrophe to pay the ransom for its liberation. It shall, then, be too late to lament: "we wish we knew."

References:

VERNON, D. and FURLOG, D., "Philosophical Foundations of AI." *DBLP* Conference Paper. DIO. 10.1007/978-3-540-77296-5_6.January, 2006. *Britanica.com*/technology/Pascaline.23/10/2024.

PART ONE

THE PHILOSOPHICAL ANTECEDENTS OF THE AI TECHNOLOGY

The Philosophical Roots of the Generative Pre-Trained Transformer Chatterbots

Stephen Omondi Owino holds a PhD in Philosophy, with a focus on Philosophy of Language. He was the Keynote Speaker and currently a lecturer of philosophy in Department of Philosophy and Religious Studies, Pwani University - Kilifi, Kenya.

Abstract

This paper examines the philosophical roots of the current Artificial Intelligence (AI) revolution brought to the fore by the launching of the open AI ChatGPT. It defends the thesis that research into the Generative Artificial Intelligence Models originated in deeply-rooted philosophical problems on the nature and role of language in the acquisition and representation of knowledge, indeed from antiquity to the present. The paper is divided into three parts: The first considers the philosophical problems raised and/or related to the AI revolution; the second traces the philosophical roots of the evolution of GPTs in the problem system of language, logic, and philosophy and, finally, it closes with an indication of new philosophical research problems posed by the emergent AI technologies.

Key Words:

OpenAI ChatGPTs: a kind of Generative AI. They specialize in the generation of texts in response to prompts. They are founded on the techniques of large language models e.g. neural network language models. The prompts provide the context.

Generative: means that they are artefacts that can create new content such as video, code, images, and text.

Pre-trained: They are trained for a period of time over a limited amount of data to allow for machine learning.

Transformer: is a stack of blocks with each block being a sheaf of neural networks which accounts for the exponential growth of parameters.

Introduction

Artificial Intelligence is a mark of another historical revolution akin to the agrarian and the industrial revolutions. It is the hallmark of the digital revolution. It is on the cutting edge, and it is cross-disciplinary. Therefore, no one can lay claim to a full mastery of its full potential. We are fortunate to be on the threshold of implementing the idea of an artefact which has a mind just like we do have. This idea is both entertaining and frightening.

It is the idea of a mechanical mind (or computational AI) which is fundamentally, philosophical and not just of advanced technology. This is clearly the case when we notice that the questions about the nature of the mind and the nature of a computer have largely been philosophical rather than scientific questions. Above all, it should not be lost to us at all from the offset, as Africans, what these cultural revolutions have portended for us in the past seven centuries.

This paper will be presented in three segments. The first part will propose some philosophical questions specific to AI, the second will attempt to show the historical link between philosophy and AI, and the third part will give a proposal towards the elaboration of philosophy of AI within the broader context of philosophy of technology.

Some Philosophical Questions Specific to AI

1) Can computers think?
2) Is there a correspondence between hardware/software distinction and mind/body distinction? And if so, is AI an affirmation of a dualist ontology that claims the existence of two different substances namely, material and immaterial?
3) Can African languages, philosophy, and cultural wisdom enjoin the Large Language Models? i.e., can we start producing stuff for AI?
4) How can we put AI into use to solve world problems from an African perspective?
5) What are the impacts of AI on education?
6) How will the evolution of AI affect human perception, cognition, and interaction?

7) What are the philosophical transformations in terms of how we understand reality and our role in it, induced by AI?
8) What will be the impact of AI on our culture, our concept of humanity, and finally, our history?
9) How are robots (or the "mechanical men") comparable to the slaves?
10) Can we have a bill of rights for the robots?
11) Is AI giving us a chance to advance from witchcraft to a scientific ontology (or metaphysics)?
12) What is the relation between minds and computers?
13) Do artificial neural networks model the brain?
14) Can Machine Learning form the basis of a learning theory?
15) What are the new conceptual structures introduced by AI to philosophical inquiry, in terms of new problems, methods, theories, and research goals?
16) Is there a philosophical uniqueness in the AI technologies?
17) Is AI providing a basis for reformulating and/or resolving the highly debatable philosophical theses in for instance, the philosophy of mind, epistemology, metaphysics, ethics, philosophy of technology, etc.?
18) What characterizes information technologies?
19) How should we model information and robotic systems?
20) How would the digital revolution impact on Africa, given that the previous technological revolutions have had adverse impacts on African societies?

Historical Link between Philosophy and AI

Logic and Language: A philosophical conundrum

In the modern period Leibniz proposed a programme for logic which would later be the inspiration towards the mathematization of logic. He proposed the creation of a universal which ought to have been a language which is maximally clear without any ambiguities and precise without any vagueness and figures of speech which are the common stock of natural languages. Vagueness, ambiguity and figurative speech render natural language inadequate for effective expression and communication of knowledge, hence the need for such an ideal language capable of clear and precise expression of knowledge.[6] The language would have basic rules of formation (*ars combinatoria*) which allow for the manipulation of the symbols of the universal language. Such manipulations or rules would be taken to correspond to the mental operations we perform in our thoughts. Finally, the language would be equipped also with rules of inference (calculus ratiocinator) which would serve as a means of calculation in order to check the validity of chains of reasoning in this language.

Even though Leibniz himself never executed his programme, it provided an ideal towards which many philosophers aspired. In the nineteenth century several mathematical philosophers, particularly, Bernard Bolzano, George Boole, Charles Sanders Pierce and Guisseppe Peano began to make progress towards the realization of Leibniz's programme. But it was the German mathematical philosopher, Gottlob Frege who brought this effort to full fruition. The system of logic outlined in his magna opus, *Begriffsschrift* (concept notation) created a symbolic system of logic with a mathematization of the concept of validity of chains of arguments which are the hallmark of modern logic. It was based on the logical constants of negation, conditional, universal quantifier and the identity relation as primitives out of which all the rest of logical operations were derived. Frege's system was powerful enough to be able to combine the following:

a. Syllogistic theory of Aristotle
b. The theory of connectives of the Stoics
c. The problem of multiple quantification that troubled the medieval philosophers
d. The theory of polyadic relations
e. Inferences involving identity

The greatest insight of Frege was that every complex expression of the system could be constructed in a stepwise process by the application of specific rules but most importantly, was that these rules do not only generate complex expressions, but they also transfer meaning from the lower level expressions to the derived expressions.

---

[6] Pierre Wagner, *La Logique*, Paris: Presses Universitaires de France, 2007 pp 6-7

This is the principle attributed to Frege known as the principle of compositionality or simply as Frege's law according to which the meaning of a complex expression is a function of the meaning of its components. The *Begriffsshcrift* in which Frege's logical system was elaborated was initially intended to describe how language is used in mathematics and to advance the logicist thesis which argues that mathematics is founded on and therefore ultimately derivable from logical concepts and principles.

But in his later writings Frege began to show particular interest in natural language by trying to see the relationship between his formal language and the natural language. In this regard he echoes Leibniz's concern that natural language is unreliable for communication of knowledge when he draws an analogy that his formal language is to natural language what a microscope is to the naked eye.[7] Other philosophers such as Bertrand Russsell, Ludwig Wittgenstein, Rudolf Carnap, Hans Reichenbach followed closely along these lines of developing and relating formal languages to natural language. This is why Frege is commonly referred to as the father of philosophy of language. However, Frege's work remained largely unknown until the contact with Bertrand Russell who took it up and gave the proposed logicism its full and complete expression in a work co-authored with Alfred North Whitehead, namely: the *Principia Mathematica*.

The *Principia Mathematica* was a monumental work and its logicist programme aroused great interests in the logical foundations of mathematics. Studies focusing on the system of *Principia Mathematica* revealed inherent weaknesses of the logicist programme. Notable among these were Godël's two incompleteness theorems. The first theorem holds that if an axiomatic system is consistent, then there is at least one theorem which can neither be proved nor disproved within the system. Mario Bunge describes such a theorem as one that is undecidable and gives the definition that "formula A is said to be *undecidable* in theory T if neither A nor $\neg$ A is a theorem of T".[8] The second theorem holds that no theory can prove itself to be consistent. This implies that it is not possible to prove a system of predicate logic

---

[7] Pierre Wagner, *Op. Cit.* p 63
[8] Mario Bunge, *Treatise on Basic Philosophy*, Vol.7, part I, Dordrecht/ Boston/ Lancaster: D. Reidel Publishing Company, 1985, p 49

to be consistent.⁹ By showing that predicate logic is undecidable Gödel concomitantly demonstrated that there is no mechanical method for testing validity of arbitrary arguments in the universal language. So, the implementation of Leibniz's programme showed at the same time that it is not fully realizable. As a consequence, to the revealed shortcomings of the system of *Principia Mathematica* logicism declined.

But while revealing the shortcomings of logicism which it was intended to defend, the *Principia Mathematica* excited enthusiasm in the direction already set by Frege of relating formal logic to natural language. Russell himself was on the forefront of this pursuit and published a popular article entitled "On Denoting." He exploited the theory of relational propositions and multiple quantification of Frege as expounded in the *Principia Mathematica* to carry out analyses of certain sentences known as the definite descriptions. His analysis reinforced the assumption that ordinary language is not only ill-equipped to deal with scientific and philosophical discourse, but it also exposed the fact that there can be tension between the logical form of expressions and their grammatical form. Failure to notice this can make language to be misleading thus lending itself to faulty logical inferences. This thesis of Russell inspired and focused philosophical attention to the close relation between logic and language thereby sparking in its wake, divergent philosophical positions with regards to the nature of the relation between the two namely, logic and language.

To some philosophers, ordinary natural languages are seen as a hindrance to clear logical thinking while for others it is unproblematic to logic. The philosophers who thought that natural language is a problem for logical reasoning proposed and embarked on the construction of artificial or ideal languages.¹⁰ Such languages are supposed to avoid or reduce the problems of ambiguity, vagueness, irregularity of meaning that is common in ordinary natural languages. Thus, every description which is intended to become part of our well-established body of knowledge should be expressed in terms of an ideal language. It is the language with capacity to articulate clearly and

---

⁹ Simon Singh, *Fermat's Last Theorem*, London: Fourth Estate, 1997, p 159

¹⁰ Rudolf Carnap was on the forefront in the attempts to construct ideal languages. Cf. Carnap, R. *The Logical Syntax of Language*, New York: Harcourt, Brace and Co.,1937

consistently a scientific body of knowledge. This is due to its structured nature in virtue of a precisely regulated formal system. The proposition for an ideal logical language raises yet another basic debate among philosophers concerned with language on the relationship between the two types of languages namely, artificial and natural. Küng has argued that while differences remain between the two types of languages, modern linguistic study carried out by linguists and logicians such as Chomsky, De Saussure, the Prague and Copenhagen schools of structuralism, among others,

> have brought to the fore the affinity between the natural languages and languages of symbolic logic, without blurring their real differences in the process...This permits the structure of natural and logistic languages to be compared more accurately than has been possible so far, so that points of agreement and difference can be precisely stated. It is, for example, interesting to compare the way in which all the sentences of the English language can be derived from several so-called kernel sentences by means of so-called transformations, with the way in which the sentences of logistic systems are formed from atomic sentences in accordance with rules of formation. Deduction rules, too, appear to be comparable to a special kind of transformations.[11]

But beyond the interests on the relation between the symbolic languages and the natural languages there is the much more basic philosophical concern on the relation between the structures of linguistic systems in general and the ontological structure of the world. This is what is called the problem of representation. The speculative grammarians[12] attempted to construct grammars purely on philosophical grounds on the assumption that there was a correspondence between grammatical categories and the ontological categories. Grammar is therefore considered as a mirror of reality and essentially the same in all languages whose differences are merely

---

[11] Guido Küng, *Ontology and the Logistic Analysis of Language*, Dordrecht-Holland: D. Reidel Publishing Company, 1967, pp 5-6

[12] The term speculative in this context does not have the current pejorative connotation of being imaginary but a specific connotation deriving from Latin "speculum" which means a mirror. Cf. D. P. Simpson, *Cassell's New Latin Dictionary*, London: Cassell and Company Ltd., 1959

accidental. The contention of the speculative grammarians was that through philosophical consideration of the true nature of things we would discover the true form of universal grammar.

As far as the artificial languages are concerned, the question of its relation to reality is much more acute given that they are artificially constructed to conform to a logical ideal guided by precise rules. Küng observes that despite the variety of these systems of logical languages they all share the commonality that they are explicitly defined by

> *definite logical and ontological views of their inventors. The translation from a natural language into a logistic language, i.e. the logistic analysis of language, involves an ontological commitment for every sentence translated. The categories of logistic signs are intended to stand in a systematical correlation to the categories in which we see the world, so that it is meaningful to investigate this correlation between the precise syntactic structures of a logistic system and the ontological structure of the world that serves it as a model.*[13]

In this view it is through the study of the structure of the artificial languages that we can come to discover the true structure of reality.

Despite the heterogeneity that might exist in these movements of philosophy, some two common elements run across them. The first is the basic assumption that natural languages are inherently unstructured and unsystematic aggregates of verbal constructions. Secondly, there is the general hostility to metaphysical speculation which they all contend that springs from the unrestrained linguistic freedom. The difference between them would originate only in their orientations aimed at addressing these two issues.

While the ideal-language philosophers and ordinary-language philosophers differed on their attitudes towards natural language, they all shared the same set of assumptions according to which natural language is unsystematic, vague, ambiguous, unstructured and misleading. However, there was at the other extreme of the spectrum, linguists who were equally well versed in logic and mathematics but proceeding from a different set of assumptions. They presupposed that language is systematic, structured, creative and therefore capable of

---

[13] Guido Küng *Op. Cit.* p 9

precise formulation. Among these are Noam Chomsky, Jerrold Katz, Jerry Fodor, Postal, Harris, Yehoshua Bar-Hillel and Montague.

Initially, these opposed sets of assumptions created a gulf between the philosophers of language and the linguists but overtime there is a convergence between the two groups. This is due to the fact that linguists are establishing theories which are of interest to philosophers, for example, the revival of the old debate between rationalists and empiricists; the nature and structure of the mind; the problems of analyticity and syntheticity; the problem of synonymy and translatability. Linguists also in turn are finding great insights from philosophers and logicians especially as they increasingly accept logical tools to analyse linguistic problems. They also receive great insights from formal philosophical semantics which they attempt to extend to the construction of natural language semantics. Consequently, the convergence of these schools of philosophy of language has created the consensus that logic and language are closely related and that logic is relevant to language only in so far as it serves to represent and formalize the part of language related to inferential thinking.

Generative Grammars

A generative grammar is a specification of a finite set of rules by means of which we can produce and recognize appropriately structured or well-formed expressions of a language.

Characteristics of a generative grammar:
a) Must generate all the well-formed syntactic structures and fail to generate any ill-formed structures.
b) Must have a finite/limited number of rules capable of generating an infinite number of well-formed structures.
c) The rules of the grammar must be recursive i.e. can be used repeatedly in generating structures.
d) Must be capable of distinguishing between deep structure and surface structure of the language.

Examples of generative grammar can be the simplest form called the phrase structure grammar and the syntax of propositional logic.

Transformational Generative Grammar's analysis

The Transformational theory in its original formulation in Chomsky,[14] conceived of grammar as solely concerned with the syntactic rules of generating all and only the well-formed sentences of a language. Syntax in this early version was seen as autonomous and entirely independent of the semantic interpretations attached to the generated sentences. Thus, a transformational theory of grammar was exclusively a theory of syntax.

But in its revised later formulations, especially as elaborated in Chomsky,[15] the transformational theory was expanded in scope to include syntax, semantic and phonology.

However, this presentation focuses only on the elementary aspects of syntax.

Briefly, a generative grammar is an explicit representation of the finite set of rules by means of which a speaker of a given language can generate an infinite set of the potential and actual well-formed sentences and not the ungrammatical ones. A transformational generative grammar is merely a further development and specification of a generative grammar that makes it (the generative grammar) more powerful and efficient to represent the rules of the language. In order to clearly grasp the notion of transformation, as it is employed in this theory, we need to draw a distinction between the surface structure and deep structure of sentences; two examples can be used to illustrate the distinction. Example one:

"John is eager to leave" (i)
"John is easy to leave" (ii)

These two sentences in their surface structures display a structural similarity analysable into subject and predicate. Yet, in their deep structures, the first sentence has "John" as the subject of the verb "to leave" while in the second sentence, "John" is the object of the same verb.

Example two: *"the shooting of the hunters was awful"*

---

[14] Noam Chomslky, *Syntactic Structures*, The Hague: Mouton, 1957

[15] Cf. Noam Chomsky, *Aspects of the Theory of Syntax*, Cambridge, Mass: MIT Press, 1965.

This is a case of a sentence with structural ambiguity. The surface structures are derived from the deep structures by means of rules, which transform them from deep to surface structures. These rules are the ones referred to as the transformational rules.

The Syntactic Component

Two sets of rules, namely the base rules and the transformational rules make up the syntactic component. The base rules are made up of phrase-structure rules and the lexicon.

Below are the phrase-structure rules taken from Chomsky[16] (1965):

1. (Sentence) ⟶ NP (noun-phrase) +VP (verb-phrase)
2. VP ⟶ Verb + NP
3. NP ⟶ NP singular
   ⟶ NP plural
4. NP ⟶ D (article) + N (noun) + 0 (Deletion rule)
5. NP plural ⟶ D+N+S
6. Verb ⟶ Aux (Auxiliary) + V (Verb)
7. Aux ⟶ Tense (Modal) (have + ing) (be + en; be + ing)

Below is a sample Lexicon

D = {the, a}

N = {man, ball ...}

V = {hit, take, walk, read, ...}

Modal = {will, can, may, shall, must}

The phrase-structure rules are rewriting rules, which involve rewriting symbols into other symbols. For example, in 1; S ⟶ NP + VP should be read as *rewrite S as NP+VP*.

---

[16] Cf. Noam Chomsky, *Aspects of the Theory of Syntax*, 1965.

ISSUES IN ARTIFICIAL INTELLIGENCE: A PHILOSOPHICAL INTERROGATION

As such what the phrase-structure rules generate are referred to as the *preterminal string*, for example NP + VP. This stands in need of another operation for rewriting symbols into actual words. The lexicon provides for this operation. It provides the primary lexical information about words, which can be appropriately applied to the preterminal strings to generate the *terminal strings* or actual sentences.

This coordination of the phrase-structure rules and the lexicon can be clearly represented in the form of a tree-diagram called *a phrase-marker*. Thus, using the phrase-structure rules and our sample lexicon, we can produce the *phrase-marker* below:

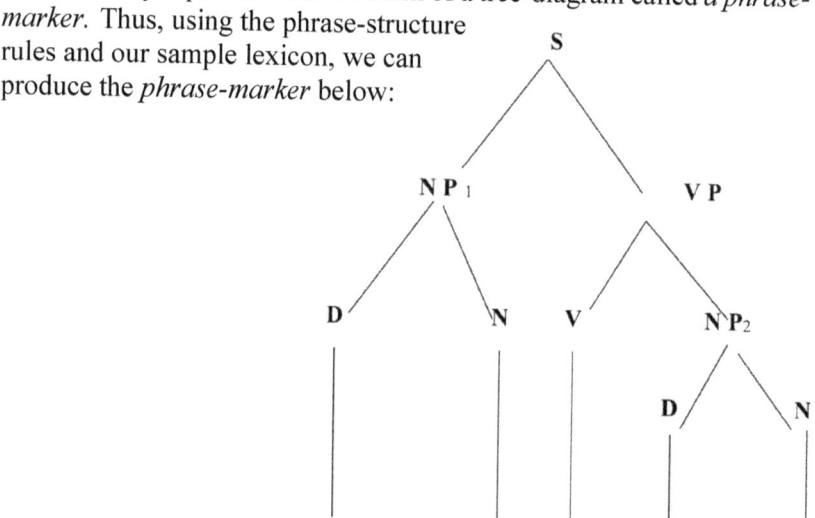

The other aspect of the syntactic component is the transformational rules. Unlike the base rules we have seen above, which operate on single symbols, the transformational rules operate on strings of symbols. As such, they apply generally to the terminal strings generated by the base rules.

For example, in our example, *the man hit the ball* when subjected to passive, imperative, interrogative and nominalization transformations would become respectively:

1   *The ball has been hit by the man* – passive
2   *Hit the ball* – imperative
3   *Has the man hit the ball?* – Interrogative
4   *The ball's being hit by the man* – Nominalization
5   *The man's hitting of the ball* – Nominalization.

For the purpose of illustration, we can take the passive and imperative cases.

The base-rule generated string is: -

NP1_____V_____NP2

The man ____ hit _____ the ball

This is the structural description (SD) and after transformation it undergoes a structural change (SC).

Passive transformation

SD: NP1_____V_____NP2

The man___hit____the ball

SC: NP2_____Aux+ be + en____v____ by + NP1[17]

The ball_____has + been _____hit_____by the man

Imperative transformation

SD: NP1_____V_____NP2

The __man___hit___the ball

SC: (deletion)_____v_____NP2

Hit_____ the ball.

In this way the transformational rules generate the surface structure of sentences which when subjected to the phonological component, give rise to the actual utterances. The base rules generate the deep structure of sentences which is operated on by the semantic interpretation of the sentences. Hence, the syntactic component provides the structural information for both the semantic and phonological interpretation.

---

[17] The "+" sign here means that (be+en) are forming parts of the auxiliary "has" and "by" is part of NP1.

The syntax of propositional logic

i) Any propositional letter, p, q, r, s, ... (with subscripts or superscripts to provide an infinite supply of variables), is a wff.
ii) If α is a wff then $\neg\alpha$ is too.
iii) If α and β are wffs then $(\alpha\wedge\beta)$, $(\alpha\vee\beta)$, $(\alpha\rightarrow\beta)$, $(\alpha\leftrightarrow\beta)$ are too.
iv) Nothing else is a wff.

Computer Program

Consider for example, the following system of rules designed to force a certain physical or chemical system to output n copies of a thing or process T upon being supplied with input S:

R1: Accept stimulus S
R2: Transform S into T
R3: Transform T into T + T
R4: Repeat (or apply) R3 n-1 times

This particular system is recursive, and it is similar to a computer programme as well as to the system of rewrite rules occurring in transformational generative grammar; neither of which is a theory proper i.e. a set of propositions closed under deduction. Instead, they are a system of rules or commands.

Language and Innate knowledge

Chomskian grammar elicited interest into the connection between language and mind. Chomsky himself claimed that linguistics *"is a sub field of psychology"*[18]

This is so because it is now expected that study of language is revealing of the things about the nature of the mind. Since, "to study language from this perspective is to study patterns of conceptualisation. Language offers a window into cognitive function, providing insights into the nature, structure and organisation of thoughts and ideas."[19] The study of language becomes as it were, a reflection of the fundamental properties and structure of the human mind thereby, giving researchers access to the design features and universal patterns of human thought.

---

[18] Noam Chomsky, *Language and Mind,* Cambridge, Mass: MIT Press, 2006.

[19] Vyvyan Evans and Melanie Green, *Cognitive Linguistics: An Introduction*, Edinburg: Edinburg University Press, 2006. p.5

Besides the proposition of an intricate relation between language and mind, philosophers have been interested in generative grammar because of its distinction between the deep and surface structure of sentences. They have felt that it would help them resolve the awkwardness that occasionally obtains between the logical form and its grammatical form. Hence the deep structure is associated with the logical form and the surface structure with the grammatical form.

But it is the question of innateness that is of philosophical interest to us i.e. the relationship between language and innate knowledge. We have observed that generative grammar is a description of rules that have been internalised by the speaker *"unconsciously"* to produce and recognize well-formed sentences.

But how it is possible for the human mind to have internalised these rules is the main issue to philosophers. Chomsky's response was that the human mind has an innate, unlearnt, complex structure. This innateness, however, has nothing to do with content but rather with the capacity to learn language. The grammars are the software as it were, that enable us to generate a language.

The mind is therefore modelled like an *Acquisition Device* capable of receiving input data and of producing some output. Thus: INPUT→ ACQUISITION DEVICE (AD)→ OUTPUT.

This is the instance of CRTT i.e. the *Computation Representation Theory of Thought* or simply known as *computationalism*. It claims that the mind is a specific type of computer with a very specific structure or "computational architecture". It is therefore the function of CRTT to specify that architecture in adequate detail. A generative grammar is therefore part of a CRTT.

Since such generative grammars have been used to model machines e.g. computers to parse natural language by simulating the human capacity to use language, it follows that such simulations reveal how the human mind operates.

The Philosophy of Technology

Technology: It is the branch of knowledge concerned with designing artefacts and processes, and with normalizing and planning human action. Traditional technology or *technics* or craftsmanship was mainly empirical, hence sometimes ineffective, at other times inefficient or worse, and only perfectible by trial and error.

Modern technology is based on science hence, it is capable of being perfected with the help of research. Main kinds: physical e.g. electrical engineering; chemical e.g. industrial chemistry; biological e.g. agronomy; biosocial e.g. normative epidemiology; epistemic e.g. artificial intelligence; and philosophical e.g. ethics, methodology, political philosophy, praxeology.

Philosophy of Technology: It refers to the ontological, epistemological and ethical study of technology. Indeed, philosophy of technology spans the entire philosophical spectrum ranging from semantics through ontology and epistemology, to axiology and ethics.

Philosophy treats technology in a broad sense ranging from engineering to decision theory. Technology is a major component of modern culture since the industrial revolution which started around 1750. Yet most philosophers have ignored technology. The few philosophers who have been concerned with technology have either sung or cursed it, for its impact on the society. These are respectively technophiles and technophobes.

Fortunately, this is changing, since it seems to have occurred to philosophers that technology represents a body of knowledge with philosophical inputs and outputs that deserve philosophical analysis just as science. This young field of philosophy is quickly growing as the conceptual richness of technology and the moral problems it raises are being recognized.

The philosophy of technology is growing in all the branches of philosophy. It is concerned with:

a) the ontological problem of the nature of the artificial
b) the epistemological problem of the peculiarities of technological knowledge and its relation to basic and applied science
c) the pragmatic (or praxiological) problem of defining the concept of rational action, i.e. action guided by designs and plans
d) the axiological problem of identifying and analysing the typical values of technology such as efficiency and reliability

e) the ethical problem of the moral codes that the various branches of technology should abide by
f) many more problems.

Of special note is the fast-growing field of **technoethics**, which is the branch of ethics that investigates moral problems raised by technology.

Philosophy and AI

We are currently living through the information revolution, which is radically and rapidly altering both the processing of information and its circulation throughout society. Information technology focuses on conceptual systems and processes for example, classification, computation, and deduction. These can now be carried out by powerful, fast and precise automatic electronic computers. Moreover, computers can now be connected to extremely complex and intricate telecommunication networks, so that they can be shared by a number of persons who can thereby have access to huge data banks leading to a worldwide socialization of information. The information revolution and its accompanying technology has therefore, two components namely, telecommunications and the computer.

In particular, the computer has posed a number of interesting philosophical questions such as: i) whether it will ever acquire all of our mental abilities; ii) whether it is the best framework to formulate a general theory of the mind.

A computer is best understood as a programmable automatic machine for processing information. Depending on the number of programmes that are fed into it a machine can become a multipurpose computer capable of carrying out a variety of tasks. Moreover, with the introduction of flexible programmes we can now produce multipurpose computers and robots that can change course automatically as they receive or produce new information.

What is philosophically problematic with computers is the very notion of a computer programme. It is a very special kind of artefact since it can be incorporated into a general-purpose computer to turn it into a special-purpose computer. Secondly, a computer programme represents and commands at the same time i.e. it is both a blueprint and an operational plan. More precisely, it can be represented by a flowchart composed of data and commands couched in some computer language.

Another point of philosophical interest about flexible programmes is that the computers capable of running them must make decisions at certain points. Of course, such decisions are not spontaneous. They are made either on the strength of the outcome of previous steps or left to chance via a built-in randomizer. This is the central characteristic of artificial intelligence.

Most certainly, the computer is a very powerful invention in the service of brains. It forces its users to think clearly, plan carefully and leave no gaps. But it can also lead to blind data gathering, in the hope that the computer will come up with the required ideas. It can reinforce the preference for quantitative accuracy over depth. It can foster the uncritical utilization of theories and models at the expense of their critical analysis as well as of the creation of new ones. The computer can also be used not to expedite creativity but to disguise the lack of it. Indeed, it can be programmed to print out useless lists, classifications, concordances and statistical correlations, as well as bogus poetry, music and visual art. In organizations it increases efficiency and eliminates much toil. But it can lead to inflexibility and unwillingness to correct mistakes or improve on operations.

These computer-induced uncritical tendencies demand attention to the AI revolution in philosophy education programmes, prompting research along two major lines namely, i) AI in philosophy education which explores the question of how we can incorporate AI tools in teaching and research in philosophy and, ii) AI education which investigates how to infuse the teaching of AI into the curricula of philosophy.

References:

ADLER, I. *Thinking Machines*, London: Dennis Dobson, 1961.

ASHBACHER, C. *Introduction to Neutrosophic Logic*, New Mexico: American Research Press 2002.

BARWISE, J. & ETCHEMENDY, J. *Language, Proof, and Logic*, Stanford, CA: CSLI Publications 2003.

BUCKNER, C. J., *From Deep Learning to Rational Machines: What the History of Philosophy can teach us about the future of Artificial Intelligence*, Oxford: Oxford University Press 2024.

BUNGE, M. *Sense and Reference*, Dordrecht: Reidel 1974a.

BUNGE, M. *Interpretation and Truth*, Dordrecht: Reidel, 1974b.

BUNGE, M "Philosophical Problems in Linguistics" in *Erkenntnis*, .1984 Vol. 21. No.2, pp. 107-173

CARTER, M. *Minds and Computers: An Introduction to the Philosophy of Artificial Intelligence*, Edinburgh: Edinburg University Press, 2007.

CHOMSKY, N. *Syntactic Structures*, The Hague: Mouton, 1957.

CHOMSKY, N. "Explanatory Models in Linguistics", in E. Nagel, P. Suppes, and A. Tarski (eds.), *Logic, Methodology, and Philosophy of Science*, Stanford: Stanford University Press, 1962, pp. 528-557

CHOMSKY, N., *Aspects of the Theory of Syntax*, Cambridge, Mass.: MIT Press, 1965.

CHOMSKY, N., *Language and Mind*, New York: Harcourt, 1972.

COREA, F., *An Introduction to Data*, London: Springer, 2019.

DAVIS, M., *The Universal Computer: The Road from Leibniz to Turing*, Newark: CRC Press, 2012.

DODIG-CRNKOVIC, G., *History of Computer Science*.

ERTEL, W., *Introduction to Artificial Intelligence*, London: Springer, 2017.

EVANS, D., *Introduction to Computing: Explorations in Language, Logic, and Machines,* (give month and date, 2011) http://computingbook.org

EVANS, V. & GREEN, M., *Cognitive Linguistics: An Introduction,* Edinburg: Edinburg University Press.

FODOR, J. D., *Semantics: Theories of Meaning in Generative Grammar*, New York: Crowell, 1977

ISSUES IN ARTIFICIAL INTELLIGENCE:
A PHILOSOPHICAL INTERROGATION

KÜNG. G., *Ontology and the Logistic Analysis of Language*, Dordrecht-Holland: D. Reidel Publishing Company, 1967

HUTTENLOCHER, D. et al., *The Age of AI*, London: John Murray, 2021.

MULLER, V. C., (ed.) *Philosophy and Theory of Artificial Intelligence*, Switzerland: Springer, 2018

PARKES, A. P., *Introduction to Languages, Machines, and Logic*, London: Springer-Verlag, 2002

PRIEST, G., *An Introduction to Non-Classical Logic*, Cambridge/New York/Melbourne/Madrid/Capetown/Singapore/Sao Paulo: Cambridge University Press, 2008

SKANSI, S., *Introduction to Deep Learning: From Logical Calculus to Artificial Intelligence*, London: Springer, 2018.

YANOFSKY, N. S., *The Outer Limits of Reason: What Science, Mathematics, and Logic Cannot Tell Us*, Cambridge, MA/London: The MIT Press, 2013.

Phenomenology of Human Subjectivity in the Hi-Tech Rationality

Anthony Ichuloi, Anthony Oure Ichuloi holds a PhD in Philosophy. He is, currently, a Senior Lecture of Philosophy at Kisii University, where he is, also, the Head of the Department of Philosophy and Religious Studies, Kisii – Kenya.

Abstract

Today, humans find themselves in a hyper technological world, which challenges their own possibilities of being, including the inevitability of their self-affirmation as a normative subjective standard of their essence. The assertion of this article is that the presence of advanced technologies in the lived-experience of the modern subject is itself an issue that challenges her being by restructuring and reconstituting it, thereby calling for a re-affirmation of her unmediated ontological role for a meaningful existence. Meaningful existence calls for a personal conscious engagement with the dominant technological rationality that threatens to annihilate human power for self-determination; it is about active engagement in the development of one's own being and destiny, which should not be relegated to technological rationality. The article argues in favour of a meaningful subjective experience. It seeks for 'human subjectivity' as a normative basis upon which technological rationality should be interpreted and measured; human subjectivity that surpasses the a priori categories of the human subject inherited from the Boethian, Cartesian and Kantian rational substance, whether mental, physical or personal, to the existentialist explanation that calls for a direct engagement with the practical world of technology that constitute human everyday concerns. In the attempts to articulate human ontology in today's hyper technological society, the discussion appropriates

Heidegger's phenomenology that gives insights into understanding of human subjectivity.

Key Words: Human Subjectivity, Hi-tech rationality, Self-affirmation, Subjective experience.

Introduction

Today, we tend to think and believe that a meaningful human subjective existence should be artificially mediated, driven and determined. This frame of thought is informed by a deliberate human choice to rely on technology to the height that almost all human activities for self-affirmation are influenced and directed by it. The deliberate choice that is informed by unconditional instrumental regard to technology, which grounds itself to the philosophy that technology is a mere instrument used to meet certain intentional ends. But then this does not tell us much about the other human reconstitutive aspect of technology. Any form of technology works at a more fundamental and phenomenological level that reconstitutes human nature, so that the instrumental question is changed along with the expected and intended answer, the need is changed along with its fulfillment. There is no doubt that technology opens up remarkable possibilities, especially in the fusion and replacement of human subjective operations as evidenced by the modern metaphysics of transhumanism (enhancement), prosthetic and biotechnology that give rise to techno-humans. For instance, in the reproductive field, *in vitro* fertilization is not simply a technology used as a means of meeting a desire to have children for those who may be having reproductive difficulties, but from an ontological level it changes the cultural and emotional frame that situates paternity, maternity, and family as a subjective component of human subjectivity.

Hyper technologies manifested through artificial intelligence have the aptitude to augment human sensory reception, emotions and cognitive abilities as well as radically enabling human health and extend life spans. However, the incontestable fact is that such technologies equally and ontologically reconstitute human subjectivity in the areas of *self-identity* and forms of *self-presentation*, thus challenging human capacity for a free thought, self-consciousness and self-determination. The fusion of humans and technology or even the replacement of human abilities for self-definition and self-presentation relegates human subjective elements to the organisation of technical rationality. The indubitable danger in all this is the possible tendency to reduce direct human engagement in the design of human destiny to making humans mere observers of their being within the technological frame of operations. It generates human subjectivities devoid of direct subjective experiences and self-affirmation for a meaningful existence.[20]

Thus, technological progress entails and presents thought-provoking issues on human subjectivity[21] that should not be left unattended, neither should they be left only to the technocrats. The entire reflection is informed by Martin Heidegger's philosophy which provides deep insights into the reality of human subjectivity in a technologically determined world, such that it affirms the dynamism of unmediated, individual subjective engagement in the disclosure of life; it goes beyond the objectifying descriptions of the human subject as a substance to be worked upon by technology or by any prearranged forces, whether mental or physical.

It is, therefore, the intent of this reflection to argue for unmediated relations of human nature amidst unrelenting mediated influence and determination of hyper technologies that are taking up human space for self-autonomy. This does not imply taking a Luddite stance on technology and the rationality it represents but rather having a conscious intent to redefine meaningfully the place of humans in the deliberately designed technological development. In appropriating Martin Heidegger's philosophic insights, the discussion advances an account of human subjectivity where humans responsibly and directly engage themselves with their own being despite the remarkable place technology takes in redefining them. To realize this, the discussion is hinged upon a series of human existential structure: *existentiality, facticity, fallen-ness, mood,* et cetera.

---

[20] Anthony Ichuloi, "A Critical Reflection on the Human Condition in Technological Development" in *Scholars Journal of Arts, Humanities and Social Sciences*, 2015, 3(3C): 745-7.
[21] The concept "human subjectivity" is used to refer to self-affirmation and active conscious human engagement with the self and with the technological world for a meaningful existence.

The Phenomenology of the "World"

The concept of the "world" raises a series of phenomenological issues that relate to human subjectivity. This is rooted in the idea that the "world" is not simply an objective reality that exists independently of humans but rather is intimately joined to human meaning. To attend to this claim, it is important to ask two basic questions: What is the world? Is the world objective or subjective, or both? These questions are grounded on the fact that, today, hi-tech rationality gives us a mechanical world that offers options for a possible actual and simulated human existence expressed through mediated relationships with things in the state of affairs. Considering the phenomenology of thinkers like Edmund Husserl and Martin Heidegger, the "world" has prominence in a real human existence, such that through it humans are challenged to show their authentic subjectivity. For these thinkers, the *world* means two basic things:

First, there is the ontical world, a pre-given world, posited by natural sciences, which is "a totality of equipment that is *"ready-to-hand"* and *"present-at-hand."*[22] It is the given, extended, physical, spatial, and measurable horizon – a *place* where human beings live, irrespective of their interests and purposes; the self-given world (basis) for human operations and experiences that is composed of extents that present and bring out the aspect of authentic human subjectivity, especially that of "care". Such that every particular assertion or negation of its constituents presupposes a perceptible material base that is there, existing in itself and capable of being grasped by exact scientific methods. This ontic world forms the objects of human perception, functions and willing at a given time as a ground for every particular experience.

Unfortunately, today, this objective world is inconsiderably infringed by science under the influence of technological rationality, turning it into a resource *standing-in-reserve* for optimization.[23] Humans transform themselves into mere *organizers* of the physical (ontic) world

---

[22]Martin Heidegger, *Being and Time,* translation by John Macquarrie, New York: Harper and Row, 1962, 123.

[23] Martin Heidegger, *The Question Concerning Technology and Other Essays,* New York: Harper and Row, 1977, 18.

while undermining the concept of *care* of the physical world as their existential structure. The profound implication of this is the reduction of humans into organizers of the technological modes of being that operate under a Cartesian philosophy that separates the physical world from human beings, so that the world is objectified as something to be ordered and manipulated. As *organizers,* humans, therefore, forsake their inner subjective relation to things in the state of affairs in order to work with the instrumental logic of technology, with no new revelation possible to arrive at the end of the technological process itself since they operate mechanically within the technological system. In such operations, human life becomes not only abstract, homeless and wordless, but also tremendously uniform, monotonous and mechanical devoid of natural underpinnings. Under such influence, all of human life and all forms of thought become epigone, scientifically provided.

The relentless technologization of the pre-given world further makes it into a mental picture. This is evidenced by the virtual realities that constitute the horizon for human self-organization – a mental representation of the real concrete world of objects, places, and activities. The ontic world is the primary source for scientific and technological determination, reconstituted into designed images of mental representation, devoid of direct human experiences. However, despite all scientific incursions into this ontic world which is the horizon in which we find ourselves consciously living, humans should be resolute to keep it and render it significant.

Second, there is the "ontological world", which is the world of human engagements and relationships, shared with other humans, entities, and in which entities derive and express their ontological significance. It is the world of shared experiences and relationships, a "lived" world rather than being observed from a distance. Since it does not have concrete determinations, the ontological world offers open and challenging possibilities of subjective human meaning. In *Basic Problems of Phenomenology*, Heidegger informs that the ontological "world is understood beforehand when objects encounter us... The mode of being of the world is not the exactness of objects; instead, the world *exists.*"[24] Heidegger's point is that the ontological world is a

---

[24] Martin Heidegger, *The Basic Problems of Phenomenology,* Indiana University Press, 1982, 10-21.

coherent, intelligible framework for human engagements and relationships for a meaningful existence, rather than a mere sum total of physical extents that come 'naturally' to us in the context of *ready-to-hand* or *present-at-hand*; it is a pre-reflective, pre-predicative human context, which at times is taken for granted. Husserl uses the concept of "life-world" to describe our meaningful engagement and structure of "acquaintedness" as aspects of authentic existence.[25]

The ontological concept of the "world" denies it being looked at as something cognitively outside, observable or inferred in terms of access with my mind as having its contents as the case with scientific investigations and technological regard.[26] And instead, it accords it a determination of human subjectivity that manifests the manner in which humans internally relate to all that explains their role in subjective experiences for self-autonomy. In Heidegger's view, the way the world is understood is reflected back ontologically upon the way in which *Dasein* itself gets interpreted.[27] While De Beistegui describes the ontological world as follows:

> ... *we exist only in and through our relation to the world, that we, as human beings are nothing independent from, and in addition to, our being-in-the-world... Openness to the world is what defines our being, not thought.*[28]

The ontological concept of the "world" introduces an important component of subjective human experience that cannot be substitued or mediated in terms or aspects of culture, beliefs, language, memories, etc. The "world" is a source of human meaningfulness, such that

---

[25] The *life-world* is the everyday world we live in with all its taken-for-granted assumptions; the world of our lived experience of the phenomena. Husserl describes it as "the world of immediate experience", "already there" and "pre-given" to us, of human concerns: of culture, art, sports, music, science, technology. Edmund Husserl, *The Crisis of European Sciences and Transcendental Phenomenology: An Introduction to Phenomenological Philosophy*, Evanston: Northwestern University Press, 1970, 379ff.

[26] David F. Krell, "The Factical Life of Dasein: From the Early Freiburg Courses to Being and Time," in *Reading Heidegger from the Start: Essays in His Earliest Thought*, edited by Theodore Kisiel and John Van Buren, New York: State University of New York Press, 1994, 371.

[27] Martin Heidegger, *Being and Time,Op Cit.*, 1962, 36.

[28] Miguel De Beistegui, *The New Heidegger*, New York: Continuum, 2005, 12.

humans do not need to refer to anything outside of themselves in terms of any objectified reality such as modern science or in terms of modern technological artefacts for the interpretation of their essence. As an internal relationship, the world reflects humans in the sense that it is absolutely part of their existential and relational structure that underlines practical their engagements as meaningful projects for subjective existence.[29] A meaningful human existence requires a movement towards interiority, a turn towards the self that characterizes the inseparability of the two worlds for a direct and immediate conscious human experience, which allows the grasp of the truth of human subjectivity in its possible and actual structure.

The notable issue is that the ontological life-world does not undermine the external predesignated, *objective* and *ontic* horizon as a basis for external subjective relationships, rather it accomplishes it within the conscious process of subjective value determinations and practical engagements, where humans in a way are constitutively world-forming agents for the fulfilment of their lives. The eminent danger of technological rationality that is defined by the objectifying Cartesian rational influence and represented in the hyper technologies is that the world is disgracefully being alienated from direct human engagements for self-autonomy. It considers the "world" not to be part of human existential structure that attests to the elements of *care* and world-forming as central elements for subjective experience and autonomy.

Today, we have the virtual world that is technologically and technically simulated or invented, devoid of its naturalness and human responsibility to it; it is a world where machines and not humans operate. Of course, there are those who argue that the technological creation of the virtual worlds does not threaten to annihilate the ontic, pre-given world of direct human experience, but rather a perfect reproduction of it.[30] But the antithesis of this is that, when technologies are conceived to operate, recreating worlds, unavoidably humans equally are made into passive developers of their own lives. Heidegger pointed out this defective technical rationality in his work "Age of the

---

[29] David Kolb, *The Critique of Pure Modernity: Hegel, Heidegger and After*, Chicago: The University of Chicago Press, 1986, 132-6.

[30] Jean Baudrillard, *The Transparency of Evil*, trans. by J. Benedict, London: Verso, 1993, 4.

World Picture" where the ontic world is turned into a mental representation or picture. Such rationality and its operations de-world the physical and ontic realities, and consequently, de-world human space for self-engagement for a meaningful existence and life. Technical rationality responsible for the creation of virtual reality has the power to obliterate human subjective role and experience, supposed to be a constitutive element for human realization and fulfilment.

A simulated world, in the ontological sense, cannot preserve the essential nature of human imprints in terms of world formation and experience. There are those who argue that it is better to experience technological virtual reality than experience no nature at all.[31] Such positions circulate scientific mismanagement of the natural pre-given world, such that it is made an object of scientific investigation, detached from the ontological concerns and responsibilities of its investigators; and that the cognitive and technical rationality is seen to be the primary way of interacting and explaining things in the ontic level of human development.[32] Conversely, the human ontological mode of being cannot be reduced to what we discover in the *ontic* inquiry, no matter how exhaustively we rationally explain the entities in the state of affairs.

When technology is given the absolute power to determine the world, then the world no longer becomes a matter of human concern and determination. To do away with the world or make it anything like a mediated reality and, therefore, a mental representation is tantamount to doing away with humans themselves. Why? Because each of us in his/her relation to the world composes his/her own unique individual self, and once that relation is destroyed, the individual is equally destroyed in her lived experience. Any attempt to alienate humans from the ontological and ontic worlds by whichever means is to render them obsolete. In other words, humans cannot be relevant outside of their conscious engagement with the world they find themselves in and form part of; they are continually challenged to have specific and unique relations to it for the meaningfulness of their existence.

---

[31] Peter H. Kahn, Rachel L. Severson, & Jolina H. Ruchert, "The Human Relation with Nature and Technological Nature", in *Current Directions in Psychological Science*, 2009, Vol.18, No.1: 338-9.

[32] Anthony Ichuloi, "A Critical Reflection on the Human Condition in Technological Development, Op Cit., 746-7.

The Human Condition in the Hi-tech World

The indisputable and indubitable fact is that technology is "inside" us, is "our world" of a lived-experience[33]; we live through, with and in it as an internal relationship and as a form of self-presentation.[34] This internal reality of technology is affirmed by the Spanish philosopher Ortega y Gasset who said that "man without technology is not man."[35] Technology has become an indispensable dimension of our being, and it is impossible today to think of being human, independent of *being-with-technology*. We are now in what Borgmann calls the regime of the *device paradigm,* where the technologies we use in our daily lives signify the kind of people we are[36], to the extent that we nolonger encounter ourselves in our essence.[37]

Amidst the indisputability of technological reality defined by technical rationality, the fundamental and most critical issue which determines human subjectivity for a meaningful existence is how we choose to attend to our being in that hi-tech world of artificial intelligence. In other words, the contestable fact in the human-technology interface is human nature (including its materiality/body) expressed in self-regard and unmediated role in its own formation and development. Today, many people opt for transhuman technologies, which paradoxically depict human nature as shapeless and incomplete, calling upon technological rationality to perfect it[38]; transhuman technologies tend to regard human nature as a conservative model of hardware that needs to be replaced or worked upon to eradicate possible

---

[33] Edmund Husserl, *The Crisis of European Sciences and Transcendental Phenomenology: An Introduction to Phenomenological Philosophy,* Op Cit., 379.

[34] Don Ihde, *Technology and the Life-world: From Garden to Earth,* Bloomington: Indiana University Press, 1990, 72-80.

[35] Ortega y Gasset, "Thoughts on Technology" in Mitcham Carl and Robert Mackey, *Philosophy and Technology: Readings in the Philosophical Problems of Technology,* New York: The Free Press, 1983, 293.

[36] Albert Borgmann, *Technology and the Character of Contemporary Life: A Philosophical Inquiry,* Chicago: University of Chicago Press, 1984, 40ff.

[37] Martin Heidegger, *The Question Concerning Technology and Other Essays,* Op Cit., 27-8.

[38] Harold W. Baillie and Timothy K. Casey, *Is Human Nature Obsolete?: Genetics, Bioengineering, and the Future of the Human Condition,* Cambridge: The MIT Press, 2005, 57-9; 73-75.

inherent deficiencies. Alexander Thomas contests that technological attempts to modify human nature under the pretext of improving it will automatically affect human dignity, especially in a manner that humans operate, it is a systemic form of dehumanization.[39] While Nick Bostrom and Kathy Cleland argue that deceitfully humans are reduced to a set of informational patterns that can be stored, manipulated and transformed for the sake of the possibility for their limitless posthuman and prosthetic human autonomy.[40] Bostrom's affirmation envision posthumans that will inhabit prosthetic bodies or live virtually as avatars in cyberspace, experiencing physical reality in the corporeal coordinates of human existence. However, Heidegger in a poetic manner asserted that "who accomplishes the challenging setting-upon through which what we call the real is revealed as standing-reserve? Obviously, man."[41]

The prosthetic conceptions of human nature would imply rooting humans from their world of direct subjective experience, such that they are conceived as not having direct individual and unmediated project or responsibility in the development of their essence; they are considered as wordless and not world-forming agents, where their responsibility to the world is relegated to external agents of technological unconcealment. This essentially challenges the place of human engagement in self-determination and affirmation. It further brings in other philosophical questions: If technology alienates humans from the project of their meaningful existence, what is the ontological content or the core phenomenon of their *being-in-the-world* of hyper technologies? Do they have any responsibility towards their own existence? Are human's integral "individuals" or "dividuals?" What is the urgent need for a techno-human paradigm shift? Why should we rethink and re-conceptualize the posthuman within the relational network of technological ontology? These questions raise an important issue of human alienation and subjugation to technical rationality, such

---

[39] Aldexander Thomas, "6: Systemic Dehumanization", in The Politics and Ethics of Transhumanism. Bristol, UK: Bristol University Press, 2024, 166-167.

[40] Nick Bostrom, "Ethical Issues for The Twenty-First Century: Transhumanist Values", in World Transhumanist Association, 2005, Vol. 1: 1-56; Kathy Cleland, Prosthetic Bodies and Virtual Cyborgs, in *Second Nature*. Issue 3, 2010: 75-6.

[41] Martin Heidegger, *The Question Concerning Technology and Other Essays,* Op Cit., 17, 27.

that uncontrolled technological development seems to promote the idea of producing, altering and marketing human subjectivity, significantly denying the fundamental role of traditional human-centered approaches that celebrate human engagement for self-development.

The intertwining of humans and technology within the frame of technical rationality subjugates humans to the relations of technological powers, where they are no longer independent of such relations. Humans lose their autonomy for self-determination to the height that their nature is conceived as an alienated beneficiary of technological development within the Platonian form of thought and implementation that undermines the physical components of human development. Technology is systematically and calculatedly designed to displace direct human mind engagement with the reality of its being, thereby becoming itself an obsolete and objectified form of engagement, devoid of any subjective contribution to its own development.[42] Some thinkers argue that a convergence of human and machine is one of the fundamental conditions for the transformation of the human self in the technological frame of evidence. Under such techno-human philosophical positions that inform modern techno-anthropology, and despite opening up possibilities to better understand the dynamism of human nature, technology should not be considered as an autonomous agency that carries its own values independent of the embodied human subject.

Any meaningful intertwine of humans and technology as expressed in trans-human philosophies should not undermine the human natural input and base. Humans should not be conceived to exist merely as beings, driven to their destiny by the inevitable powers of technical rationality rather are the centre of technological developments. Any form of technology should be at the service of man; it should not be purposed to substitute him. In other words, although it is comprehensible to think that human existence does not take place in a vacuum, the issue of a meaningful human involvement in defining his/her own being is fundamental, particularly in *being-in* or *in-ness* in a technological world and determination.

---

[42] Harold W. Baillie and Timothy K. Casey, *Is Human Nature Obsolete?: Genetics, Bioengineering, and the Future of the Human Condition*, Op Cit., 57-9; 73-75.

In the Heideggerian context, *in-ness* is primarily a matter of a positive engagement or involvement with our existence; a kind of a conscious active residing or *dwelling* in the technological reality[43], such that existence itself becomes a meaningful human task. It is possible to realize this task even within human involvement with technology so long as humans themselves are conscious of their relationship with it. The basis of *in-ness* is having human experiences of the world of technology by being *open-to-it*, directing it and disclosing-it, without consigning this subjective task to technological disclosure.[44] In other words, *being-in-the-technological* world is an ontological task to humans who embrace it and not vice-versa. In the Heideggarian phenomenology, entities like robots with human characteristics that take up human subjective responsibilities should be understood as being *within-the-world* and not *being-in-the-world* of human engagement for meaning. As a human subject, *am-in-the-world* of technology, fundamentally with a different mode of existence than the way robots or any other entities are *in-the-world*. Why? Because I, with my sensational body, consciously experience and relate with the world of technology; robots as mechanical technological gadgets do not experience anything, and they do not ask fundamental questions about their mode of *being-in-the-world* of their own specific and related technologies.

Virtualization of reality under the pretext of human quest for mediated way of life undermines direct human conscious experience, which consequently leads to multitude of paradoxical human relational possibilities devoid of actual concrete relational subjects. I am aware that there are those who contend that it is plausible to assume a simulated consciousness, but when human reality, including bodily experience is entirely removed from the background, it equally makes human choices, freedoms and actions inauthentic. In the face of virtual bodies/reality, our physical bodies have been removed out of their role in human meaning. A decorporealised subjectivity lacks direct

---

[43] Mark Wrathall and Jeff Malpas, *Heidegger, Authenticity, and Modernity: Essays in Honour of Hubert L. Dreyfus, Vol. I*, London, Cambridge: The MIT Press, 2000, 209-10.

[44] Johnson Puthenpurackal, *Heidegger Through Authentic Totality to Total Authenticity*, Leuven: Leuven University Press, 1987, 83-4.

participation for self-realization and development.[45] This is in agreement with Barlow, who noted: "Suddenly, I don't have a body anymore .... I have been reduced to a point of view."[46] In other words, prosthetic technologies outspread our bodies beyond their cognition and subjective experiences, thus undermining existential human engagements that are within the spheres of concrete individual experiential possibilities of human operations for subjective meaningful existences. For instance, today with prosthetic bodies, if I want to move my limbs and experience myself as a unity, through technology I will have to do it with a press of a button. But this is a denial of the phenomenological body as a source of my sensory perception and feedback. In its profound sense, prosthetic technology and the philosophy informing it, threatens to bestialise the pre-given traditional metaphysics of human nature that recognizes the place of the body and direct self-participation in one's development. Machines may simulate a perfect reality for humans, but then this would be unrealistic since they generate merely objectified simulated experiences and not actual authentic and concrete ones that are imperative qualifiers of human subjectivity.

Another fundamental characteristic of *in-ness* that humans constantly project in their experience is that of *revealing* or *unconcealment* of the ontological significance of entities within the ontic world for a meaningful human existence.[47] Nothing else in the world, not even technology itself has the ability to disclose entities in terms of their significance. In the Heideggerian consideration, this is called *lumen naturale*[48], which means both *light* and *clearing* in the woods. In the clearing in the woods, there is a place where there are no trees and the sunlight can reach the ground, so that things are revealed or shown to us as "mattering," attractive, useful, and sometimes as threatening, which is equally important. In the clearing in the woods,

---

[45] Ingrid Scheibler, "Heidegger and the Rhetoric of Submission: Technology and Passivity," in *Rethinking Technologies*, edited by Verena Andermatt Conley, Minneapolis: University of Minnesota Press, 1993, 127.

[46] David H. Barlow, "Unraveling the mysteries of anxiety and its disorders from the perspective of emotion theory" in *American Psychologist, 2000, 55*(11), 1247–1263.

[47] Zain Ridling, *A Comprehensive Study of Heidegger's Thought*, New Orleans, Louisiana: Columbus University Press, 2001, 28.

[48] Martin Heidegger, *Being and Time*, Op Cit., 171.

you can see the grass, the surrounding trees, bushes, birds singing, animals roaming around, etc. Heidegger describes the *clearing* as:

> *Beyond what is, not away from it but before it, there is still something else that happens. In the midst of beings as a whole an open place occurs. There is a clearing, lighting.... This open centre is ... not surrounded by what is; rather, the lighting centre itself encircles all that is.... Only these clearing grants and guarantees to human beings a passage to those entities that we ourselves are not, and access to the being that we ourselves are.*[49]

Humans are like clearing in the woods. They have the capacity to make entities known and allow them to realize their ontological relevance and role. As *lumen naturale*, "humans are disclosedness," so that without embodied human beings there will be just the woods.[50] For example, when I enter a room or any environment, I bring with me the capacity to experience through my body all that is around me, and things get revealed to me in their essences and purposes. I disclose them in their ontological significance. This is what human subjectivity is all about. It is this ontological relationship humans have with entities within the world that makes the world meaningful for us and in itself. In the technological society, technology has become the way of revealing entities, but the analogy Heidegger uses means that entities *within-the-world* do not reveal me as a human subject. Instead, I the human subject, am like a *clearing* in the woods; that is, my being as a human subject is to disclose the significant entities of my experience, including technological objects.

Revealing/clearing, therefore, is entering into a particular relationship, where reality manifests itself in a specific way as meaningful, such that it is determined by the specific relation we have with it.[51] There is no doubt that the world of hyper technologies appears to be given to us independently of our own individual choices, such that

---

[49] Martin Heidegger, *Discourse On Thinking*, translation by John M. Anderson and Hans E. Freud, New York: Harper and Row, 1966, 39-40.

[50] Walter A. Brogan, *Heidegger and Aristotle: The Two-foldness of Being*, New York: State University Press, 2005, 156.

[51] Peter-Paul Verbeek, 2005, *What Things Do*, Pennsylvania: The Pennsylvania State University Press, 2005, 50.

we find ourselves in it, and it is also true that we buy specific technological products with certain specific roles that are supposed to help us to realize our own, individually determined ends. But the incontestable fact is that the technologies we employ are constantly changing the concept of human nature as unconcealment; it creates a discrepancy between the technological nature, subject to its mediation, revealing, augmentation, simulation of human revealing and human unconcealment that allows the ontological meaning of the world to manifest.

Thus, techno-human reality is a split of the ontology of human subjectivity because it disengages humans from their direct personal responsibility that opens up areas of self-expression for a meaningful responsible task-based existence.

Human Subjective Existential Structures in the Technological Frame

The concept of *clearing* in the woods discussed in the preceding subsections introduces important structures of human subjectivity: *existentiality, moods, distantiality, facticity, language, anxiety,* and *care*. In Heideggerian phenomenology, these structures are unique and constitutive ways that entail human involvement in defining their place in the world that apparently is now being manipulated by hyper technologies. Only three of the mentioned existential structures will be discussed in this reflection: *existentiality, moods, and distentiality/fallenness*.

Existentiality

In the Heideggerian phenomenology, existentiality is the projection of possibilities of disclosing the ontological significance of entities; it simply means *understanding*. Heidegger explains that "understanding is the existential Being of *Dasein's* own potentiality-for-Being; and it is so in such a way that this Being discloses in itself what its Being is capable of".[52] This means that *existentiality* is not a

---

[52] Martin Heidegger, *Being and Time*, Op Cit., 184.

matter of understanding through a priori abstractions or through powerful technologies that enhance human knowledge in the cognitive, epistemological and psychologistic sense or is it to ask philosophical questions about the existence of reality.[53] Rather, it is an act of personal and meaningful engagement with objects of our experience. It is connected with the idea of practical engagements and possibilities in human-object interactions.[54] For instance, when I understand what a table is, it is not because when I walk into a room and I see an object with a round top and metal or wooden legs, decorations all over, and from sense data I infer that it is a table. Rather, the question in my mind is: What can I do with a table? A table by a functional definition, is what I can use for studying, eating, writing on, placing valuables on, etc. The fact that I can do something with the object (for eating, for placing valuables, etc.) is because I am already familiar with tables in terms of their purposes or relevance; I understand the table in terms of what can be done with it in my practical experience. Heidegger says:

> *The work which we chiefly encounter in our concernful dealings-the work to be found when one is 'at work' on something, has a usability which belongs to it essentially; in this usability it lets us encounter already the "towards-which" for which it is usable.*[55]

Whenever I have a *ready-to-hand* relation to technological objects, those objects should become my practical world in that their ontology reciprocally contributes to my human enablement to the height that I cannot relate to them from a detached, objectified and un-relational standpoint. Such a relationship should be constructed and organized through what those entities ontologically serve for human meaningful existence or life. The most important aspect of this is that it brings together the objects of our external world, and the inner-dimension of our subjective experience for a meaningful life. The understanding of the world is based on the possible ways that the various objects, tools, and other humans around me are related or relate to each other and to me, and I constantly project contexts of possibilities

---

[53] Mark Wrathall, *How to Read Heidegger*, London: Granta Books, 2005, 41-44.

[54] Martin Heidegger, *Being and Time,* Op Cit., Johnson Puthenpurackal, *Heidegger Through Authentic Totality to Total Authenticity,* Op Cit., 15-18

[55] Heidegger, 1962, *Being and Time,*Op Cit., 197.

in which the various objects of experiences are revealed to me. Objects in our daily world are what they are because of the way they fit into a specific context of what can be done with them in the future, in terms of significance to their users.[56] They form an internal relation to the users, and therefore, are never objectified nor perceived to have external relations to their users. Michael Zimmerman in his commentary on Heidegger's tool analysis explains this saying:

All the elements in the work world are internally related. There is no such a thing as an isolated tool; tools occur within an equipmental-referential context in terms of which a particular thing can reveal itself as a tool. Without this meaningful referential context, this familiar domain in which we have lived from the start, this 'world,' tools could not be.[57]

Humans understand things, tools or objects including technological gadgets through their possibilities of use, and those possibilities have to do with meaningful human future. In other words, understanding is always oriented towards the context of future possibilities for humans, pointing towards possible actions and possible experiences that can be had with objects of human use in the future. When I understand an object as *ready-to-hand*, I demonstrate not only its priori categories, but also, and above all, the context or "world" that gives its ontological relevance (or lack thereof). In effect, to exist as humans means always to be absorbed in practical tasks of disclosing entities; we are manifest beings.[58] Mark Wrathall asserts this saying that "our experience of the world is pervaded by an understanding of what things are, or how they are to their users"[59], while Andrew Feenberg reiterates that knowledge is ultimately rooted in the enactment of practical meanings in everyday experiences.[60]

---

[56] Thomas Sheehan, "Dasein", in *A Companion to Heidegger*, edited by Hubert L. Dreyfus and Mark A. Wrathall, Malden, MA: Blackwell Publishing, 2005, 197-204.

[57] Michael Zimmerman, *Heidegger's Confrontation with Modernity: Technology, Politics, Art,* Bloomington: Indiana University Press, 1990, 139.

[58] Martin Heidegger, *Being and Time*, Op Cit., 182.

[59] Mark Wrathall, *How to Read Heidegger*, Op Cit., 41.

[60] Andrew Feenberg, *Between Reason and Experience: Essays in Technology and Modernity*, London, Cambridge: The MIT Press, 2010, 193.

The destruction of ontologically unmediated role of human beings has a tremendous impact on the way in which humans conceive of themselves and give form to their own existence and the being of other entities; it works against humans themselves threatening their individual subjectivities through the destruction or elimination of the necessary direct connection between them and the world of their engagement. The technological forces transform or mechanize experience of the self and of the life-world for human meaning, delinking humans from their fundamental role and internal relation to themselves and to the world. Technological forces *alienate* humans from their own disclosive comportment towards reality and towards themselves and consequently reconstituted into mere spectators of their own lives, where life is seen as a series of events occurring outside of oneself. Hefner affirms this impact of hi-tech culture when he says that technology rearranges both our world and perceptions of our own human nature[61], such that a primal unity and wholeness of human life is adversely challenged to its disappearance.[62]

The phenomenology of *understanding* as an existential human structure that responsibly engages humans with their environment is, consequently, the opposite of Descartes and Kant, who explain understanding in terms of abstract a priori categories, where the mind organizes the physical world of perceptions and sensations in accordance with reason devoid of practical engagement with it. Further, it rejects the alienating and theoretical Cartesian and Kantian dualism inherited by modern science and technology that makes a sharp and seemingly irreconcilable distinction between humans and the objects of their practical lives. In today's technologically determined society, humans are challenged to return to *things themselves*, not as data in human consciousness as is the case with Husserl, but rather to things as mediated by direct unmediated human experience; humans are not merely thinking substances, contemplating objects or alongside-objects. They are *beings in the world* of meaningful concerns for both entities in the state of affairs and themselves.

Whereas technologies are expected to enhance human nature, helping to positively enhance human meaning, now the reality is that they

---

[61] Philip Hefner, *Technology and Human Becoming*, Minneapolis: Fortress Press, 2003, 12.
[62] Charles Guignon, *On Being Authentic*, London and New York: Routledge, 2004, 50.

are ruining it. Modern technical rationality tends to undermine the fact that humans have a specific ontological role to play in the un-concealment of things in the state of affairs. Human ontological duty of *un-concealment/revealing* has been exclusively taken over by scientific and technological *revealing*, turning humans into mere spectators of techno-human *revealing* or *disclosure*. But then, this creates the sense of a pre-given or *ontic* self and the world out there for us to refer to and master to the height that between us and the objective reality, electronic magnetic processes that we do not even understand are powerfully at work.

Therefore, existentiality defines humans as engaged *world-revealing* and *world-forming* subjects. Its destruction by any medium equally implies the destruction of humans themselves. Attempts to reconstitute subjective human concerns for self-realization to technological determinations will, disgracefully, make the human role for self-determination obsolete. It is a subversion of the human subject since it gives rise to techno-humans, with technology being its first nature. Techno-humans lack, in themselves, the autonomy and the knowledge proper to self-consciousness. However, the fusion of technical rationality with humans should constantly challenge us to rediscover and relocate our natural-subjective role in shaping and determining our unmediated nature.

Moods

Moods are a constitutive internal state of human subjectivity that relate humans to their subjective and objective worlds. Martin Heidegger explains that our *understanding* of the being of objects *within-the-world* is grounded on our state of mind or mood.[63] He further adds that "mood has already disclosed, in every case, *being-in-the-world* as a whole, and makes it possible first of all to direct oneself towards something."[64] The argument is that moods designate emotional rationality of human engagement for meaningful existential ways of relating to ourselves, others and to our world of experience. They are

---

[63] Martin Heidegger, *Being and Time,* Op Cit., 76.
[64] Ibid., 176.

ways of 'coping' with reality since they relate to specific human purposes, thereby fundamentally deepening our experience of things.[65]

Moods engage, disclose, and tune us into experiencing the world in a particular and unique way, since they give subjective insights that enhance our meaningful experience of life.[66] Reiterating the ontological importance of moods, William Large argues that, unlike intellectual knowledge that directs itself to particular objects and persons in the world, through moods we can know what matters to us as directed by our feelings, passion, interests, love, etc.[67] In so doing we come to know what the world looks like and how it is for us; moods define the way the world affects us, and how it matters to us in a way that could not happen with a mere theoretical understanding of the same world.[68] Since the world matters to us, we are passionately concerned about it by developing an interest in experiencing it as mediated by our moods as an internal relation that does not just tell us about how we understand the world outside there; but also also show how things are going on with us and within us.[69]

The thinking that moods orient our understanding of the world should not be construed to mean a yearning for a merely nostalgic and pre-ontological level of consciousness, uninterrupted by the mechanical rhythms of technology, but rather it is an ontological rethinking of the fundamental importance of moods in determining human subjectivity. Today, with the deep intrusion of scientific and the highly sophisticated technological calculative thinking, we try to control our moods, treating them as external, thereby undermining their ontological value in human

---

[65] Hubert Dreyfus, *Being-in-the-World: A Commentary on Heidegger's Being and Time, Division I*, London-Cambridge: MIT Press, 1991, 170-8.

[66] Carman Taylor, Foreword to 'What is Metaphysics?' in Martin Heidegger, *Basic Writings: From Being and Time (1927) to The Task of Thinking (1964)*, edited by David Farrell Krell, London and New York, Routledge Classics, 2011, 43-44.

[67] William Large, *Heidegger's Being and Time*, Bloomington and Indianapolis: Indiana University Press, 2001, 58-9.

[68] Greaves Tom, *Starting with Heidegger*, New York: Continuum International Publishing Group, 2010, 66-8.

[69] Michael Zimmerman, *Heidegger's Confrontation with Modernity: Technology, Politics, Art*, Bloomington: Indiana University Press, 1990, 141; Hubert Dryfus, *Being-in-the-World: A Commentary on Heidegger's Being and Time, Division I*, Op Cit., 174.

nature. This, consequently, leads to detached technological interpretations of the human subject, which leads to the perversity of the human condition. It leads to a mechanistic mode of existence, where humans are alienated from their own internal emotional and phenomenal relation and experience of the world for a meaningful life. With technological mediation, amplified by hyper-relational technologies, humans engage their moods unreflectively to the height that as fundamental and internal aspects for a creative, subjective experience, moods are constantly manipulated, undermined, and rendered obsolete and irrelevant. This, in essence, destroys unmediated and affective individual involvement with whatever is the object and subject of human experience.

There is no doubt that today, technical rationality fascinates us, it captivates our moods, and we are enticed to use technological gadgets as external mediums to express our relationship with reality, to a point where sometimes we are not able to have a deeper ontological and subjective attachments to things, including ourselves in the natural world. Hyper technologies have the power to positively and negatively reconstitute moods/emotions. For instance, individuals often use computers and related devices to mediate their personal intimate relationships, thus influencing their emotions in social spheres of interactions. It is indubitable that different technologies not only extend our bodies and actions in space, but also our feelings; artificial intelligence can magnify emotions and feelings to the point that it brings closer the time one spends with another and intensifies the feelings. For instance, the iPod/iPhone has not only revolutionized the personal handheld device industry, but the very space of our senses. When I listen to an iPod, the music I desire follows me everywhere I go. In this way, the seduction of the iPod stems from the fact that it allows me to craft everything auditory: I can store more data and easily carry, navigate and choose sounds with its visual display and its miniature size. Through the iPod, I instantly exchange the noise and chaos of the street for an auditory space of my own choosing.

With reconstructed feelings, the spheres of human emotional experiences are equally mechanically reconstructed. Most intimate and meaningful emotional desires are now replaced by technological machines, thereby creating what can be called techno-feelings or techno-moods that do not have subjective underpinings. However, a desire to build better relationships with, and through technological relational mediations should take into account the quality of the implied relationships, such that the influence of human feelings is truly involved for authentic individual self-contribution and manifestation in that relationship. For example, lonely people, today, go online when they feel depressed, anxious, or desire emotional support. The online medium benefits them by allowing them to have positive experiences of engaging in virtual social interactions with constructed identities in the online context.[70] To enhance and keep such online virtual relations, profile creators continually construct and present more desirable, attractive versions of the virtual individual selves to attract online users. Instead of being their authentic selves, the created profiles project the selves that the online users desire and would like to become. This in itself a common strategy to break up from face-to-face emotional confrontation interaction, which some may argue to have nothing wrong. But going online as remedy to emotional social decadence is itself inability to face the truth and the fact of oneself and one's loneliness in the relational human structure. In agreement with Sherry Turkle, since people invest themselves emotionally into relational technologies without careful consideration, we may end up demeaning the basic intimate relationships that define and express ourselves as relational beings in the social sphere.[71]

Constructed techno-emotions have the ability to desensitize humans and create an emotional relational gap between the real subjective world and the virtual objective relational world. It further diminishes and deludes our specific and unique emotional ability to genuinely relate to ourselves and to things that are happening around us in the state of affairs. Instead of living lives guided by sentiments for a more challenging and meaningful human development, technology incessantly reproduces vapid, virtual versions of identities and feelings and, calculatedly through adverts, entices humans to consume them. But, since technologically constructed moods are subject to

---

[70] Ju-Yu-Yen., Cheng-Fang Yen., Cheng-Shung Chen., Peng-Wei Wang., Yi-Hsin Chang, & Chih-Hung K, Social Anxiety in Online and Real-life Interaction and their Associated Factors, in *Cyberpsychology, Behavior, and Social Networking*, Vol. 15, No.1, 2012: 9ff.

[71] Sherry Turkle, The Tethered Self: Technology Reinvents Intimacy and Solitude, in *Continuing Higher Education Review*, Vol. 75, 2011, 30.

manipulation, ontologically they do not enable humans to engage in a naturally creative manner with the world of their subjective experience; they are disaffecting abstractions of the emotional self. Technology has the aptitude to manipulate the mood-sphere of human structure by increasing transient sensations and redirecting them so much that humans no longer sense or imagine *from within* or see their affective reality as it is through their unmediated experiences.

Therefore, since technologies are sometimes used to manipulate feelings and human identities neither think nor feel, traditional metaphysics of embodied human nature or subjectivity should be considered indispensable and irreplaceable. Moods or feelings should not be construed as a kind of transient internal weather, where we feel this now and in one hour or so we feel differently, or that I am sad right now and sooner or later I will be happy. Rather, they are to be taken as internal and fundamental aspects of subjective experience that renders human reality present and meaningful because they engage humans in tasks that are unique to them, thereby exclusively defining their subjective existence.

Falling or Distantiality

Falling or distantiality is a crucial structure of human subjectivity, particularly in everyday human existence in a hi-tech society.[72] Heidegger uses the term "fallen-ness" to describe the negative manner in which humans are occupied with everyday tasks, thus avoiding to confront some basic issues that affect them. In fallen-ness humans move away from the subject-object relation as their fundamental human existential structure to object-subject relation to the height that in their everyday *being-with, they* look to *others* and to some external reality in the material world for the affirmation of the meaning of their being.[73] In such subjugation, they stop asking themselves *basic questions* about their own existence. Falling is uncritical, naïve and *inauthentic* identification with things *within-the-world*, where we tend to understand ourselves through present objects and subjects (other

---

[72] Johnson Puthenpurackal, *Heidegger Through Authentic Totality to Total Authenticity*, Op Cit., 32-4; Zaine Ridling, *A Comprehensive Study of Heidegger's Thought*, New Orleans, Louisiana: Columbus University Press, 2001, 29.

[73] Martin Heidegger, *Being and Time*, Op Cit., 164.

people) in the world, and through pre-given models presented to us by the social and material contexts in which we find ourselves. Today, it is almost assumed normal to be identified with what we *have* and *do*, and not with who we actually *are*; that is, with our being. In the context of technological determination, we get overwhelmed by our technologies and identify ourselves with them as is the case with transhuman technologies that give rise to techno-humans.[74]

Today, humans get absorbed or immersed in the *they-self* of technologies that they are interested in as attempts to give meaning and purpose to their lives and existence; they unconsciously regard themselves mere users/consumers, who exist to accomplish technological goals independent of their own self-interests. It is a way of going along with the crowd of technological rationality and simulations, living only in the eyes and mercy of technology without a profound reflection on the possible negative consequences posited by such technological relations. Humans become dependent upon what is external to them (technological devices), denying themselves the ability and possibility to determine their destiny. Consequently, they lose control of what the techno-device public presents to them, thereby surrendering themselves to its forces and losing their own subjective power for self-determination. Heidegger, observes this fallen nature of humans in the technological frame noting that "it seems as though man everywhere and always encounters only himself… In truth, however, precisely nowhere does man today any longer encounter himself, i.e., his essence."[75]

The elusive nature of technological rationality, calculatedly makes humans incapable of giving direction and orientation to it, including their own self-encounter in the human-technology engagement process; humans appear to have totally lost autonomous control of their technologies, which conversely has come to control them. Inevitably, this is experienced with Nano-technologies that today have become powerful structures and forms of self-presentation, thus

---

[74] Don Ihde, *Heidegger's Technologies: Post-phenomenological Perspectives*, New York: Fordham University Press, 2010, 31-2.

[75] Martin Heidegger, *The Question Concerning Technology and Other Essays*, Op Cit., 27.

fundamentally altering the human subject's whole being.[76] Such technologies are not just discrete forms of modern subjective mediated experiences, rather, they have also gained autonomy over the modern subject's self-determining character.[77] Nano-technologies render the human subject powerless in the face of his/her own life to the level that she begins to identify herself with them. The example of technological influence, within the frame of fallen-ness, is that of the automobile. Automobile ownership today involves far more than transportation: it symbolizes the owner's status in society. In poor contexts, it has even greater symbolic meaning than in rich ones, signifying the achievement of modernity and its vision of a rich and fulfilling life. In such cases, the automobile that is meant to be a means has turned out to shape identities, making humans incapable of encountering themselves – their own selfhood.

Charles Guignon, affirms the human condition under the influence of technical rationality saying that, "as inauthentic selves, we tend to drift into socially approved slots and accept everything at face value without any sense of the deeper origins of our possibilities."[78] In his later work, he adds that "with the coming of the disenchanted outlook of modernity, a primal unity and wholeness of life has been lost"[79]. The argument here is that technological rationality brought by artificial intelligence tends to decide roles, standards and norms, including how humans are understood and interpreted; that is, on the basis of human practical and "concernful" absorption in the world of technological rationality. For instance, transhuman technologies, with their embedded philosophies influence the manner of shaping human subjectivities, such that humans are compelled not of their choice to adapt and accept what is technologically presented to them as the most ideal form of self-presentation.

---

[76] Ernst Schraube, "Torturing Things Until they Confess": Günther Anders' Critique of Technology, *Science as Culture*, Vol 14, No.1, (2005), 77-85.

[77] Langdon Winner, *Autonomous Technology: Techniques-out-of-Control as a Theme in Political Thought*, Cambridge, MA: MIT Press, 1977, 57.

[78] Charles Guignon, *Heidegger and the Problem of Knowledge*, Indianapolis: Hackett Publishing Company, 1983, 138.

[79] Charles Guignon, *On Being Authentic*, Op Cit., 50.

Thus, *fallen-ness* as a human existential structure is unreflective and inauthentic mode of existence, where humans are made to think and belief that their self-realization revolves around what is other than themselves, adopting a kind of outward-looking approach to their existence and life; they constantly turn away from the truth of themselves and their own existence to what science and technology present to them. But this external relation should challenge us to return to ourselves, to our subjectivities in search of the meaning of our existence that cannot be encountered in the trusted technological frame. However, as informed by Jacques Ellul[80], once facing the ceaseless pursuit of efficiency through artificial intelligence, humans must be made to yield to their subjectivity, as they opt to yield their bodies and brains to technological rationality.

However, the fundamental questions to ask are: Is the intentional shift to technology, especially artificial intelligence not a form of self-alienation or *self-distance?* Are humans not alienating themselves from their essence? The basis for these questions is that the existential structures of human subjectivity analysed in the preceding sections, are being taken away from humans by technological rationality or AI and technically used as a power to oppose or fight against the very humans in a manner of de-skilling or disabling them by creating a situation of dependency on such a technology. When basic human structures are tampered with, *self-alienation* becomes an inevitable loss of human identity and subjective experiences for meaning, which in itself is a warning to complete trust of humans to technology. In other words, the implementation of technological rationality has today become the inward embedded force that fight against humans themselves, uprooting them from their ontological ground for self-presentation.

Conclusion

In this work, an attempt has been made to elaborate a phenomenology of human subjectivity in a technologically determined

---

[80] Jacques Ellul, *The Technological Society*, translation by John Wilkinson, New York: Vintage Books, 1964, 115; *Ibidem,* "The Technical Order", *Philosophy and Technology: Readings in the Philosophical Problems of Technology*, edited by Carl Mitcham and Robert Mackey, London: The Free Press, 1972, 85-87.

rationality. It has accentuated the paradoxical nature of the development of technology. On one side, it positively enhances humans, and on the other hand, it undermines the ability of humans themselves to individually in unmediated manner work for their own destiny. It has underlined some unique and important existential human structures that are constantly threatened and challenged by the reality of hyper technologies; that technology tends to obscure human subjective roles in the self-development process.

The reflection has also attempted to give a positive non-scientific and non-technological account of the human subject, whose essence consists in no less than his/her openness to the ontological significance of his/her being in search of a responsible self-account kind of existence in the world of his/her everyday concerns. Humans should consciously engage themselves with the world of technology and take their existences as a project, a self-directed project that calls for their own active and practical engagement in taking it to realization. Such a subjective project cannot entirely be left to the determinations of external technological agencies, which in their own right tend to substitute basic human experiences with technologically mediated experience. Technologically mediated experience undermines the human subject's subjective role and responsibility for self-development in the context of self-fulfilment and realization. As humans uphold the use of technology to enhance their abilities and externalize their goals, they should be conscious of preserving human aspects that manifest the uniqueness and irreplaceability of human nature.

The discussion has exhorted a turn to the human subjective self, which should be a genuine basis for self-autonomy in a technologically en-framed world that relentlessly challenges human power for self-determination. A return to the human subject is a call to reflect on what it is to be truly a human subject within the reconstituting power of hi-tech rationality. Humans do not just have an external and technologically driven nature but fundamentally have internal self-determining nature that should be upheld. Unreflective embracement of technical rationality will lead humans into finding themselves displaced from their autonomous ontological task to technological manipulation.

References:

BAILLIE W. Harold and CASEY K. Timothy, *Is Human Nature Obsolete?: Genetics, Bioengineering, and the Future of the Human Condition*, Cambridge: The MIT Press, 2005.

BARLOW, H. David, "Unraveling the mysteries of anxiety and its disorders from the perspective of emotion theory" in *American Psychologist*, 2000, 55(11), 1247–1263.

BAUDRILLARD, Jean, *The Transparency of Evil*, translation by J. Benedict, London: Verso, 1993.

BERGHOFER Philip, *The Phenomenological Critique of Mathematisation and the Question of Responsibility: Formalisation and the Life-World* by Ľubica Učník, Ivan Chvatík, Anita Williams (Eds.), Springer, 2015.

BOELLSTORFF, Tom, *Coming of Age in Second Life: An Anthropologist Explores the Virtually Human*. Princeton: Princeton University, 2008.

BORGMANN Albert, *Technology and the Character of Contemporary Life: A Philosophical Inquiry*, Chicago: University of Chicago Press, 1984.

BOSTROM Nick, "Ethical Issues for The Twenty-First Century: Transhumanist Values", in *World Transhumanist Association*, 2005, Vol. 1: 1-56.

BROGAN A. Walter, *Heidegger and Aristotle: The Two-foldness of Being*, New York: State University Press, 2005.

CLELAND, Kathy, Prosthetic Bodies and Virtual Cyborgs. In *Second Nature*. Issue 3, 2020: 74-101

DE BEISTEGUI Miguel, *The New Heidegger*, New York: Continuum, 2005.

DREYFUS Hubert, *Being-in-the-World: A Commentary on Heidegger's Being and Time, Division I*, London-Cambridge: MIT Press, 1991.

ELLUL Jacques, "The Technological Order", in Mitcham Carl and Robert Mackey, *Philosophy and Technology: Readings in the Philosophical Problems of Technology*, New York: The Free Press, 1983.

FEENBERG Andrew, *Between Reason and Experience: Essays in Technology and Modernity*, London: The MIT Press Cambridge, 2010.

GERSHON, I. (2010). *The Breakup 2.0: Disconnecting over New Media*. Ithaca: Cornell University.

GREAVES Tom, *Starting with Heidegger*, New York: Continuum International Publishing Group, 2010.

GUIGNON Charles, *Heidegger and the Problem of Knowledge.* Indianapolis: Hackett Publishing Company, 1993.

GUIGNON Charles, *On Being Authentic.* London and New York: Routledge, 2004.

HEFNER Philip, *Technology and Human Becoming.* Minneapolis: Fortress Press, 2003.

HEIDEGGER Martin, *Being and Time.* Translation by John Macquarrie, New York: Harper and Raw, 1962.

_____, *Discourse On Thinking.* Translation by John M. Anderson and Hans E. Freud, New York: Harper and Raw, 1966.

_____, *The Question Concerning Technology and Other Essays.* New York: Harper & Row Publishers, Inc., 1977.

_____, *The Basic Problems of Phenomenology.* 2nd edition by Albert Hofstadter, Bloomington: Indiana Press, 1982.

_____, *The Metaphysical Foundations of Logic.* Translation by Michael Heim, Bloomington and Indianapolis: Indiana University Press, 1984.

_____, *The Fundamental Concepts of Metaphysics: World, Finitude and Solitude.* Translation by William McNeil and Walker, Bloomington and Indianapolis: Indiana University Press, 1985.

HUSSERL Edmund, *The Crisis of European Sciences and Transcendental Phenomenology: An Introduction to Phenomenological Philosophy.* Evanstan: Northwestern University Press, 1970.

ICHULOI Anthony, "A Critical Reflection on the Human Condition in Technological Development" in *Scholars Journal of Arts, Humanities and Social Sciences*, 2015, 3(3C): 743-752.

_____, "A Response to the 'Enframing' Nature of Modern Technology. *International Journal in IT and Engineering"*, 20215, Vol.3, Issue 11, 17-30.

_____, *Modern Science and Technology, a Challenge to Human Self-understanding,* Scholars' Press, 2016.

_____, "The Reconstituting Nature of Modern Technology on Environment" in *The International Journal of Humanities and Social Studies,* 2015, Vol 3 Issue 6, 314-421.

IHDE Don, *Technology and the Life-world: From Garden to Earth.* Bloomington: Indiana University Press, 1990.

_____, *Bodies in Technology*. Minneapolis: University of Minnesota, 2001.

KAHN, H. Peter, Severson L. Rachel, & Ruchert H. Jolina, "The Human Relation with Nature and Technological Nature", in *Current Directions in Psychological Science*, 2009, Vol.18, No.1: 37-42.

KOLB David, *The Critique of Pure Modernity: Hegel, Heidegger and After*, Chicago: The University of Chicago Press, 1986.

KRELL F. David, "The Factical Life of Dasein: From the Early Freiburg Courses to Being and Time" in *Reading Heidegger from the Start: Essays in His Earliest Thought*, edited by Theodore Kisiel and John Van Buren, New York: State University of New York Press, 1994.

LARGE, William, *Heidegger's Being and Time*. Bloomington and Indianapolis: Indiana University Press, 2001.

ORTEGA Y GASSET, José, "Thoughts on Technology", in Mitcham Carl and Robert Mackey, *Philosophy and Technology: Readings in the Philosophical Problems of Technology*, New York: The Free Press, 1983.

PUTHENPURACKAL, J. Johnson, *Heidegger through Authentic Totality to Total Authenticity*. Leuven: Leuven University Press, 1987.

RIDLING, Zaine, *A Comprehensive Study of Heidegger's Thought*. New Orleans, Louisiana: Columbus University Press, 2001.

SCHRAUBE, Ernst. "Torturing Things Until the Confess: Günther Anders' Critique of Technology," in *Science as Culture, Vol 14, 1,* (2005), 77-85.

SHEEHAN, Thomas, "Dasein", in *A Companion to Heidegger*, edited by Dreyfus, and Wrathall, Malden, MA Blackwell publishing, 2005.

THOMAS, Alexander, "6: Systemic Dehumanization", in *The Politics and Ethics of Transhumanism*. Bristol, UK: Bristol University Press, 2024.

TURKLE, Sherry. (2011). The Tethered Self: Technology Reinvents Intimacy and Solitude, in *Continuing Higher Education Review*, Vol. 75, 2011, 30

_____, *Alone Together: Why we expect More from Technology and Less from Each Other*. New York: Basic Books, 2011.

VERBEEK, Peter-Paul, *What Things Do*. Pennsylvania: The Pennsylvania University Press, 2005.

_____, *Moralizing Technology: Understanding and Designing the Morality of Things*. The University of Chicago Press, 2011.

WINNER Langlong, *Autonomous Technology: Techniques-out-of-Control as a Theme in Political Thought*. Cambridge, MA: MIT Press, 1977.

WRATHALL Mark and MALPAS Jeff, *Heidegger, Authenticity, and Modernity: Essays in Honour of Hubert L. Dreyfus, Vol. I*. London-Cambridge: MIT Press, 2000.

WRATHALL Mark, *How to Read Heidegger*. London: Granta Books, 2005.

YEN, J.Yu., YEN, C. Fang., CHEN, C. Sheng., WANG, P. Wei., CHANG, Y. Hsin., & KO, H. Chih, "Social Anxiety in Online and Real-life Interaction and their Associated Factors", in *Cyberpsychology, Behavior, and Social Networking*, Vol. 15, No.1: 2012, 1–12.

ZIMMERMAN, Michael, *Heidegger's Confrontation with Modernity: Technology, Politics, Art*. Bloomington: Indiana University Pres, 1990.

PART TWO

AI AND THE EPISTEMOLOGICAL QUESTIONS

A Critical Evaluation of Lonergan's Concept of Human Understanding and Artificial Intelligence (AI)

Gerard Nnamuga, CSSp, holds a PhD in Theology, with a focus on Systematic Theology and Biblical Theology. He is a Full-Time Lecturer at Tangaza Institute of Philosophy and Theology (TIPT), in Nairobi – Kenya.

Abstract

This paper is a comparative study between Lonergan's concept of human understanding and Artificial Intelligence (AI). Drawing from Lonergan's work entitled Insight[81] and particularly his concept of human knowing, I will show that AI is grounded in human intelligence. The overall thrust of this paper's argument is the recognition that artificial intelligence has many functional advantages, which from the face of it, seem to outstrip human capabilities in accuracy, precision, complexity and speed. Yet AI still lacks the most fundamental aspects of intelligence: agency and flexibility, which are products of insight and understanding, which only human intelligence is capable of. However complex AI activities might be, insight and understanding, and the possibility of thinking outside the box are impossible for it. Despite the speed by which AI performs its actions and the troves of data it possesses, it depends on human intelligence. Our approach to AI, this paper argues is to avoid the two extremes of overestimating its achievements on the one hand and the other to be too cautious of its limitations.

Key Words: Human Understanding, Artificial Intelligence, Insight, Data and Lonergan, John McCarthy.

---

[81] Bernard J. F. Lonergan, *Insight: A Study of Human Understanding*, (New York: Philosophical Library, 1957).

Introduction

Bernard Joseph Francis Lonergan *(1904 –1984)* was born on 17 December 1904 in Buckingham, Quebec, Canada. Between 1922 and 1937 he studied for four years at Loyola College, Montreal, and entered the Society of Jesus in Guelph, Ontario. From 1926 to 1930 he studied philosophy, languages, and mathematics at Heythrop College, University of London, England. He did theological studies at the Gregorian University, Rome, from 1933 to 1937. He was ordained a priest in 1936, while still at the Gregorian University, and graduated with a doctorate in 1939. He wrote two important works, *Insight: A Study of Human Understanding* (mainly for Philosophy) and *Method* (mainly for Theology).

His book, *Insight* presents his version of Aquinas' philosophy of knowing from a contemporary perspective. His task is to understand 'what it is to understand.' He focuses primarily on the knower, and secondly, on the known. He begins the study of understanding considering the 'dramatic instance' illustrated by Archimedes rushing naked from the bath at Syracuse crying 'Eureka!'. With this instance, Lonergan gives to the reader "an insight on insight" and introduces the characterization of this important concept. I will dwell on Archimedes' insight as a point of intersection between Lonergan and AI because the journey to insight began with an inquiry, seeking to know. Archimedes did a lot of research before he arrived at that moment of joy. John McCarthy too who coined the phrase Artificial Intelligence did a lot of research before he created a computer programme that mimics human intelligence. At the same time, I will insist that AI cannot supersede human intelligence, the creator and designer of AI as the example of driving a car illustrates.

I will begin this investigation with the advantages and disadvantages of firstly, AI and secondly, human intelligence. Then I will delve into the process of human knowing articulated by Lonergan's *Insight*. This process, according to Lonergan starts with questioning and proceeds to experiencing outer and inner sensing, imagining and remembering.

Advantages and Disadvantages of Artificial Intelligence and Human Intelligence

The phrase "Artificial Intelligence" (AI) was first coined by John McCarthy[82] in a project proposal to the Rockefeller Foundation for funds to do research "Dartmouth Summer Research Project on Artificial Intelligence", dated September 2, 1955. John McCarthy describes Artificial Intelligence as follows:

"Every aspect of learning or any other feature of intelligence can in principle be so precisely described that a machine can be made to simulate it. An attempt will be made to find how to make machines use language, form abstractions, and concepts, solve kinds of problems now reserved for humans, and improve themselves."[83]

Today, Artificial intelligence is described as the performance of tasks normally requiring human intelligence processes by machines, especially computer systems. Everything can be considered AI if it involves a program doing something that we would normally think would rely on the intelligence of a human being. Specific applications of AI include visual perception, speech recognition, translation between languages, and expert systems.

Advantages of Artificial Intelligence

Speed

A computer can perform thousands if not millions of operations in a second. This is a huge advantage when searching for matches, calculating numbers, and checking alternatives. Using AI alongside other technologies we can make machines make decisions faster than humans and carry out actions quicker. While making a decision, human beings will spend time analysing many emotional and practical factors.

---

[82] https://www.kaggle.com/discussions/general/246669
[83] Suni Kumar, *"Advantages and Disadvantages of Artificial Intelligence"*, Medium. https://towardsdatascience.com/advantages-and-disadvantages-of-artificial-intelligence-182a5ef6588c. Accessed on May 4, 2024. This article is also published in *Towards Data Science*, November 25, 2019.

However, an AI-powered machine works on what is programmed and delivers the results at a very fast speed.

Accuracy and Precision

One of the biggest benefits of Artificial Intelligence is that it can significantly reduce human errors and increase accuracy and precision. Artificial intelligence takes decisions from the previously gathered information by applying a certain set of algorithms. So, errors are reduced and the chance of reaching accuracy with a greater degree of precision is increased. When programmed properly, errors can be significantly reduced to null. An example of the reduction in human error through AI is the use of robotic surgery systems, which can perform complex procedures with precision and accuracy, reducing the risk of human error and improving patient safety in healthcare.

Memory

There is almost no limit to the amount of data memory that can be attached to artificial intelligence. Chess databases can include every high-level game ever played. An example is Deep Blue, the IBM chess program that beat Garry Kasparov in the 1990s. Deep Blue can identify pieces on a chessboard and make predictions, but because it has no memory, it cannot use past experiences to inform future ones.

Complexity

Artificial intelligence can deal with many variables at the same time. Models of climate change, landing a Boeing 747, connecting buyers and sellers all over the globe, multiple inputs and outputs can be handled speedily and accurately.

Risks

This is a great advantage of AI. We can overcome many risky limitations of humans by developing an AI Robot and drones which in turn can do dangerous things for us. For example, drones are used in wars, robots are going to Mars, defusing bombs, exploring the deepest parts of oceans, or mining for coal and oil. They can be used effectively in any kind of natural or man-made disaster. The Chornobyl nuclear power plant explosion in Ukraine happened at a time when there were no AI-powered robots that could help minimise the effect of radiation by controlling the fire in the early stages because any human being who would go close to the core would die in a matter of minutes. They had to sand and boron from helicopters from a distance. Today, self-driven drones are used in wars.

Always Available

An average human being will work between 4 and 6 hours a day excluding breaks. But with AI we can make machines work all the time of the day without any breaks, and without getting bored, unlike humans. An example of this is online customer support chatbots, which can provide instant assistance to customers anytime, anywhere. Using AI and natural language processing, chatbots can answer common questions, resolve issues, and escalate complex problems to human agents, ensuring seamless customer service around the clock.

Digital Assistance

Highly advanced organizations use digital assistants to interact with users which saves the need for human resources. Digital assistants are also used in many websites to provide things that users want. We can chat with them about what we are looking for. Some chatbots are designed in such a way that it's become hard to determine whether we're chatting with a chatbot or a human being.

AI is open to indefinite improvement along these lines and utilising these strengths. However, there are distinct limitations.

Limitations of Artificial Intelligence

Quantifiable Data

All data must be quantifiable. AI has to be reduced to electronic positive or negative, on or off, one or zero. In the end, artificial intelligence is a mechanical processing of electronic impulses.

Passive

Artificial intelligence is passive. It follows rules and does what the software program tells it to do. If you want to design a computer to learn, you must put in a program to tell it: 'if it works do it again; if it does not work do something else', or similar instructions. The instructions are the software programs, the algorithms used, the hardware, and the executive files.

Lack of Initiative

Computers will never take initiative unless they are programmed to do so. Talk of the morality of robotic behaviour is misplaced. It is the programmers of the robots, who are the moral agents. Volkswagen designers, administrators and manufacturers were morally responsible for cheating on emissions tests; no one in their right mind would indict the computers.

Unemployment

As AI is replacing the majority of the repetitive tasks and other works with robots. Human interference is becoming less, which is likely to cause major problems for the meaning and value of human labour. Every organization is looking to replace the minimum qualified individuals with AI robots that can do similar work with more efficiency.

High costs

The ability to create a machine that can simulate human intelligence is no small feat. It requires plenty of time and resources and can cost a huge deal of money. AI also needs to operate on the latest hardware and software to stay updated and meet the latest requirements, thus making it quite costly.

Lacking Out-of-Box Thinking

Machines can perform only those tasks which they are designed or programmed to do, anything out of that they tend to crash or give irrelevant outputs which could be a major backdrop.

Therefore, Artificial intelligence will always retain the character of passivity, mechanical, and following the rules of the software.

Advantages of Human Intelligence

Whatever 'intelligence' we attribute to computers and artificial intelligence, it is but a pale reflection of the human intelligence of the inventor, the designer, the manufacturer and the user.

Rich, Multi-layered and Complex

Human Intelligence involves questioning, experiencing, understanding, interpreting, recognising, getting ideas, judging true or false, correct or incorrect, good or bad; we decide and implement our decisions.

Infinitely Flexible

Human Intelligence is capable of thinking, doing, and making all things. We can ask questions about everything. We can think of and understand all things in varying degrees. We can develop in-depth, width, detail, wisdom, and learn. Human intelligence operates in terms of understanding causes, relations, identities, characteristics, ideas, laws, regularities, and anticipations. And then being able to apply that understanding to a unique situation. We take this all for granted.

Active and Creative

We have invented languages, we have discovered technologies, we have constructed libraries, we have specialized in the sciences and generalized our philosophies. We have cultures, values, moral laws and religious aspirations. We have arts, music, and politics. We are conscious, responsible, actively thinking and doing.

Development

For the individual, it develops from childhood to high school, to university, to adulthood, to maturity, to the wisdom of old age. For the cultures, our understanding advances through the sciences, through applied technologies, to deeper and wider understanding, through discoveries, experiments and new data from new instruments.

Limitations of Human Intelligence

Firstly, Human intelligence is slow because thinking takes time. Secondly, humans have limited memory which decreases with age. Thirdly, humans can deal with one or two variables at a time. We have limited ability to deal with complexity.

Despite these limitations, human intelligence still has enormous advantages over AI. Computers have never asked questions, never got ideas, never interpreted or recognized anything, never conceived the implementation of an idea, and never produced instruments to help it. Computers are mechanical and passive as opposed to humans who are actively intelligent, creative, and developing, whose conscious intelligence encompasses all the causes, laws, regularities, and systems of the universe.

Lonergan's Insight and Artificial Intelligence

Genuine dialogue is based on similarities and differences. Both Bernard Lonergan and AI have a common ground which offers a fruitful ground for dialogue and enrichment. Bernard Lonergan a well-known philosopher and theologian emphasizes the process of knowledge and cognition. AI is the performance of tasks normally requiring human intelligence processes by machines, especially computer systems. It is clear from these descriptions that the intersection between Bernard Lonergan and AI is that both deal with processes of human knowledge and understanding. The difference between the two is that Lonergan offers the theoretical framework but AI offers the practical structure. We have already seen the advantages and disadvantages of AI. I am going to offer an overview of Lonergan's process of human knowledge before I delve into the areas of intersection.

Insight: A Study of Human Understanding (1957)

The key idea of this monumental book is the act of insight. Lonergan elaborates on the full development of human intelligence and human knowing. Human knowing starts with questioning, proceeds to experiencing outer and inner sensing and imagining and remembering, then to the five characteristics of direct insight, description and explanation, images to ideas, distinguishing true and false ideas, and evaluating and applying the truths.

The task Lonergan sought to accomplish in Insight was to understand 'what to understand is' by primarily focusing on the act of knowing and secondarily on that which is known. He says: "Thoroughly understand what is to understand, and not only will you understand the broad lines of all there is to be understood but also you will possess a fixed base, an invariant pattern, opening upon all further developments of understanding."[84]

His philosophy unfolds in the answers to the following three questions: Firstly, What am I doing when I am knowing? Second, Why do I do the act of knowing? Third, What do I know when I do it? The answers to those questions result in a cognitional theory, an epistemology and a metaphysics, respectively.

He asked these questions for two reasons:

Firstly, to provide what he called a "common ground" on which people could meet one another, that is, the common ground of the operations through which they pursue meaning and truth.

Secondly, to provide a solution to the fragmentation of knowledge—not by attempting to integrate the content of knowledge, but by acknowledging the same operations of experiencing, understanding, and judging in all fields.

This acknowledgement, which Lonergan demonstrates in *Insight*, brings a startling unity to knowledge and the pursuit of understanding in every field. It helps us relate such "hard sciences" as mathematics, physics, and chemistry to the sciences of life, and to relate all of these to psychology, philosophy, the arts, and theology.

Lonergan re-examines the Thomistic experience-understanding-judgment view of human knowing, with the insistence on understanding the role of the observer as a key to valid knowledge. He calls for a

---

[84] Lonergan, *Insight*, xxviii.

method, accepted and employed, in theology and philosophy, comparing the scientific method on the one hand, and the structures of mathematics on the other, resulting in his empirical and inductive method. It is the inductive method which Lonergan uses that offers an important link to AI.

Lonergan in Dialogue with AI

According to Lonergan, human learning begins with the development of insights. Insights are moments of heightened awareness and understanding that arise through a process of inquiry and reflection. They represent a shift in perspective, allowing individuals to grasp the underlying patterns and principles that govern a particular subject matter. Insight enables individuals to move beyond mere accumulation of information and fosters deeper understanding.

He begins the study on insight by considering the 'dramatic instance' illustrated by Archimedes rushing naked from the bathroom crying 'Eureka!'.[85] With this instance, Lonergan gives the reader "an insight on insight" and introduces the characterization of this important concept. Archimedes after a long time of research and experiments arrived at the principle that the upward buoyant force that is exerted on a body immersed in a fluid, whether fully or partially, is equal to the weight of the fluid that the body displaces. This insight and discovery came suddenly and unexpectedly. Lonergan says "Archimedes had his insight thinking about the crown; we shall have ours by thinking about Archimedes."[86] He continues to say that insight hinges on five fundamental factors:[87] firstly, it comes as a release of the tension of inquiry, secondly, it comes suddenly and unexpectedly, thirdly, it is a function not of outer circumstances but inner conditions, fourthly, it pivots between the concrete and abstract and fifthly, it passes into the habitual texture of one's mind. Let us dwell on two of these characteristics of insight.

---

[85] Lonergan, *Insight*, 1.

[86] Lonergan, *Insight*, 3.

[87] Lonergan, *Insight*, 3-4.

Insight Comes as a Release of the Tension of Inquiry

Archimedes' release of the tension and outburst came after an inquiry. This inquiry for a long time, involved research, and experiments. It started with the desire to know, to understand and to see why, to discover the reason for and to find out the cause of. This has been the trademark of the scientific method, thus doing experiments, arriving at theories, and developing them into laws. One insight leads to another insight by applying the scientific method.

One of the fastest-growing scientific innovations is AI. It has grown in leaps and bounds over the last 70 years since John McCarthy coined the phrase "Artificial Intelligence". This one too started with an inquiry to know and discover. He might not have had an outburst like Archimedes but felt some satisfaction to see that at last he had got it and also paved a road map for AI's development up to 2015. After serious research, John McCarthy invented a computer programming language known as LISP based on the mathematical theory of recursive functions (in which a function appears in its own definition). It is interesting to note that Lonergan too began his reflection on insight by mathematics and mathematical physics, because, according to him, mathematicians know exactly what they are doing when they have insights. His goal was to have an insight into insight. Through inquiry and research, AI has increased exponentially.

Insight Passes into the Habitual Texture of One's Mind

Lonergan uses the phrase "the habitual texture of one's mind"[88] which means that insight passes into the habitual texture of the mind. In other words, we take it for granted and act accordingly. It seems to be very easy for a human to drive a car. But that is only because the building blocks have been put in place over the years of experiencing, experimenting, remembering, coordinating, judging speed, distance, visibility, interpreting signs, and all the skills we take for granted. After all, we are intelligent. Lonergan gives an example of a bicycle. When one learns how to ride it, it becomes a habitual act. Basing on Lonergan's example, let us look at a self-driven car and show how driving it brings out the essential difference between Human Intelligence and AI.

---

[88] Lonergan, *Insight*, 6.

Self-Driving Cars

Before Archimedes could solve his problem, he needed inspiration, but he no longer needed it once the solution was found. A difficult problem becomes simple. And tends to remain simple. This characteristic makes learning possible. What one really understands somehow becomes part of one's own being. It is like riding a bike. After this characterization of insight, Lonergan discusses the genesis of the definition of a circle and the insight-involving cognitive process that allows one to go from a cartwheel to the concept of the circle. The question now is: can artificial intelligence mimic human intelligence to the extent that self-driving cars can interact smoothly with human drivers in the rough and tumble of our imperfect road system? Let us compare how the human person brings human understanding and deciding to bear on driving and ask, is it possible for artificial intelligence to emulate these skills?

Autonomous vehicles as they are now called can keep a vehicle in a lane, correctly change lanes, and speed, but the requirement is still there that the driver MUST always be ready to intervene if the computer makes a mistake. The function of the computer is to recognize that the driver is not paying attention and to sound the alarm.

The human driver is a smooth integration of consciously, paying attention, seeing, understanding, recognizing, judging, deciding and acting. Human understanding has no difficulty because it can understand rules, situations, things, and conditions; can judge the relevance of each to a unique time and place and can decide appropriately and immediately.

Humans understand the rules of the road. The rules are ideas; they are abstract and general. But each motoring situation is concrete and particular and unique. Human intelligence is again needed to recognize the situations where the rules apply; to recognize which rule takes priority over others; and in the end, to judge what is the right thing to do; and to do it. Because human understanding is flexible, it can cope with emergencies, the unpredictable, the unique, the unexpected, and the exceptions that prove the rule. To understand is to grasp an idea, to recognize an instantiation of that idea, and to adapt driving to the requirements of the situation. Humans can easily recognize and adapt to conditions of rain, snow, slippery surfaces, urban driving, highway driving, pitted roads, and day or night driving.

AI actually understands nothing, never has, and never will. AI does not consciously see, does not recognize, does not interpret, does not judge. All it does is follow the rules of software programs responding to electronic input from various sensors. A program is needed to recognize a person, another to recognize a set of lights, another to recognize a hydrant, another to recognize a bicycle, and so on. There seem to have been three accidents with autonomous vehicles. One crashed into the back of a truck in front of it on the highway; it did not see or recognize a truck in plain sight. Another killed a pedestrian crossing the road with her bicycle; another ran into a wall. Humans because of our intelligence take for granted the ability to recognize these things, situations, contexts, and conditions. But for artificial intelligence, a special program has to be created for each of these particular elements. AI does not have the ability to apply general rules to particular situations without a further software program to tell it how to do it. Mega data does not solve the problem: it just gives you more and more particular examples but never a general idea with the ability to apply it to any unique situation.

A further difficulty for artificial intelligence is that input from sensors is limited; you may not see the whole of the pedestrian or of the other car, or of the bicycle. Tests on high-security sites on the Internet sometimes ask you to identify any picture with a part of a car in it. A human can do this; it is very difficult for a computer or robot to do that. Very often in driving you just see the front of a car protruding from an exit, or part of a pedestrian obscured by a parked car, or a sign obscured by a high truck in front of you.

Humans understand humans; human drivers understand other drivers and can usually understand their intentions or predicaments. In a controlled and quantifiable environment such as a chess board or conveyor belt, the computer will excel. AI has a future in controlled situations such as factories, robotics, computers, and dealing with large-scale data. The driving environment is not controlled or structured; it is full of complications, exceptions, unique situations, unpredictable behaviour, human wisdom and human folly. AI is not good in such an environment. There is no room for error on the road; lives are at stake.

And because human lives are involved, what looks simple for Human Intelligence due to the habitual texture of one's mind is extremely difficult for AI to mimic.

There is a certain hubris that artificial intelligence can solve all our problems. Autonomous vehicles are attempting to mimic human intelligence, but ironically manufacturers do not seem to have a clue about how human intelligence works. In the end, AI can only be as 'intelligent' as the intelligent, creative, human designer manufacturer and user makes it to be.

Conclusion

Bernard Lonergan's ideas on human learning emphasize the importance of self-awareness, critical thinking, and the role of experience in acquiring knowledge. AI has significantly influenced the perception of knowledge by enhancing access to information, providing personalized learning experiences, enabling data analysis, and transforming the job market. However, ethical and philosophical considerations remain crucial as we navigate the complex interplay between AI and human learning. It is essential to harness AI's potential while preserving the uniquely human capacities for self-reflection, critical inquiry, and the pursuit of wisdom.

References:

LONERGAN, Bernard J. F. *Insight: A Study of Human Understanding*, New York: Philosophical Library, 1957.

_____, *Insight: A Study of Human Understanding*. In: *Collected Works of Bernard Lonergan*, 5th ed., ed. F. E. Crowe and R. M. Doran. Toronto: University of Toronto Press, 1992, vol. 3, 27-770.

_____, *Method in Theology*, London: Darton and Longman and Todd, 1971

MORELLI Mark D, and MORELLI, Elizabeth A. *The Lonergan Reader*. Toronto: University of Toronto Press, 1997.

TEKIPPE, Terry J. *What is Lonergan up to in Insight?: A Primer*, Collegeville, MN: The Liturgical Press, 1996.

The Abyss between Human and Artificial Intelligence

John Mundua, AJ., holds a PhD in Philosophy, with a focus on Philosophical Anthropology. He is, currently, Lecturer of Philosophy at the Apostles of Jesus Institute of Philosophy and Theology (AJIPT), and a Part-time Lecturer at Tangaza Institute of Philosophy and Theology (TIPT).

Abstract

Literature on artificial intelligence can be sampled into different genres, among such genres, are two of which hold opposite positions. On the one hand, is artificial intelligence triumphalism, which promises the creation of a superintelligence, aiding the artificial enhancement of human intelligence. Its central belief is that enhanced human intelligence will solve human problems to a level that is unprecedented in human history. On the other hand, there is the artificial intelligence apocalypse, which predicts the extinction of human intelligence as it fuses with or gets replaced by artificial intelligence, which will soon become more potent than human intelligence. Accordingly, then, artificial intelligence will set up human intelligence on an irreversible path of extinction. The first position prepares us to await digital triumphalism, whereas the second position sparks the dread of the future of the advancement of the technology of artificial intelligence, as it predicts the catastrophic replacement of humans with artificial super-humans (like robots), in all spheres of human activities. This study views the two positions as unwarranted exaggerations. It argues that there is an abyss between human and artificial intelligence such that, the fusion of human intelligence into or replacement by artificial intelligence to form a superintelligence is utopian and therefore characterises those who await digital triumphalism as just awaiting the Godot. At the same time, it argues that the claim that human intelligence can be set by artificial intelligence for extinction is impossible because human intelligence is an intentional embodied consciousness, which artificial intelligence is not.

Key Words: Artificial, human, intentionality, embodiment, consciousness.

Introduction

This study is divided into four parts. The first part gives an overview of artificial intelligence, pointing out its two forms. It points out the main claim of strong artificial intelligence, which the study sets out to dispute in the subsequent parts. The main argument of the study is that artificial intelligence cannot replicate human intelligence because the latter is an embodied intentional consciousness. The subsequent parts offer discussions of the qualities of human intelligence as embodied, conscious and intentional. The second part discusses the embodiment of human intelligence and its significance in explaining the difference between artificial and human intelligence. It uses the theory of embodiment of the French phenomenologist Merleau-Ponty to set the main arguments. The conclusion of the second part is that, it is impossible to replicate human intelligence in artefact by simulation as in computers because such artefacts are not lived bodies. The third part discusses consciousness as uniquely a characteristic of human intelligence that can only be analogized to artificial intelligence. Otherwise, artificial intelligence cannot replicate human intelligence on account of consciousness that cannot be created artificially. The fourth part discusses intentionality as another characteristic element that is unique to human intelligence. Its conclusion is that, much as artificial intelligence can mimic the computational character of the mind, it cannot mimic intentionality in human intelligence, because such intentionality is linked to consciousness and lived experience.

Artificial Intelligence: An Overview

The phrase Artificial Intelligence was coined by John McCarthy.[89] It highlights two concepts, namely, intelligence and artificial (used as an adjective) that can lead us to understand its literal meaning. We can define artificial intelligence according to the meaning intended by McCarthy as, the replication of intellectual processes characteristic of human cognitive activities such as generalization, data analysis, and reasoning, in digital computer artefacts (like robots). It is the simulation of certain aspects of the processes at the intellectual level of human cognitive operation. Cognitive scientists analyse the human mind and view it as a computational system. Artificial intelligence is the mimicking of the complex computational functioning of the human mind through algorithms and programs. In a nutshell, artificial intelligence is the replication of the working of the mind in a computational nonbiological substrate.[90]

Searle categorizes artificial intelligence into two forms, namely, weak and strong artificial intelligence. The distinguishing feature between the two is the claim that they individually hold about their comparison to human intelligence. According to Searle, weak artificial intelligence lays a claim of being instrumental in the execution of human intelligence, such that, it is understood as a tool used to perform tasks with serious rigour and precision, which otherwise human intelligence cannot handle.[91] Thus, weak artificial intelligence is the mimicking and application of intelligent human behaviour, applied in a limited sense just as a perfect tool for solving complex problems. It does not lay any claim of a parallel sentient and conscious intelligence to that of humans.[92] Strong artificial intelligence, for is part, is claimed to be

---

[89] John R. Searle, "Can Computers Think?" in *Philosophy of Mind: Classical and Contemporary Readings*, David J. Chalmers ed., (New York: Oxford University Press, 2002), 670.

[90] Murray Shanahan, *The Technological Singularity* (Massachusetts: MIT Press, 2015), 15.

[91] John R. Searle, "Minds, Brains and Programs", Behavioural and Brain Sciences", in *Philosophy of Mind: Contemporary Readings*, Timothy O'Connor and David Robb, eds. (New York: Routledge, 2003), 332.

[92] Danial Sonik and Alessandro Colarossi, *Becoming Artificial: A Philosophical Exploration into Artificial Intelligence and What It means to be Human* (London: Imprint Academic Ltd, 2020), 27.

not merely a tool but equated to operations of human mind because it exhibits exactly the cognitive state and operations of the human mind. Thus, strong artificial intelligence is a creation of fully conscious entity from computational programs and hardware.[93] According to the proponents of strong artificial intelligence, a computer is not merely a tool but rather a mind when appropriately programmed.[94] Thus, strong artificial intelligence is claimed to have understood and other cognitive states that are found in human intelligence. It is argued that if a computer is appropriately programmed, it can literally have a cognitive state similar to that of humans and can operate just like the human mind, perhaps even better. The claim of strong artificial intelligence draws attention to reflect on the psychological and philosophical significance of simulation of the cognitive activities and capacities.

This study refutes the claims of strong artificial intelligence that sentience and consciousness can be artificially created and described in algorithmic forms, while appreciating weak artificial intelligence and its contributions to the betterment of human life. For example, in the contemporary world, weak artificial intelligence is employed in algorithmic computations that allows extremely high-speed data processing and analysis, used in identification and correlation of patterns, which are then employed for prediction of future events. Weak artificial intelligence is also being massively employed in a wide range of sectors e.g. in healthcare where it is used for medical diagnosis, and finance where banks use it for predictive analysis to help make very fast decisions in trade and investment. However, the claim of strong artificial intelligence that it can replicate human intelligence is refuted in this study. In the sections that follow we discuss how artificial and human intelligences are worlds apart and the two as separated by an abyss. What renders strong artificial intelligence incapable to replicate human intelligence is that the latter is embodied, conscious, and intentional.

---

[93] Danial Sonik and Alessandro Colarossi, *Becoming Artificial*, 27.

[94] John R. Searle, "Minds, Brains, and Programs" in *Introduction to Philosophy: Classical and Contemporary Readings*, John Perry and Michael Bratman, eds. (New York: Oxford University Press, 1999), 368.

Embodiment of Human Intelligence

To demonstrate that to claim to create intelligence artificially is an exercise in futility, we need to turn to examine embodiment and the exercise of embodied consciousness, which is uniquely present in human beings.[95] Human intelligence is a product of the human body's interaction with the environment. This environment can be physical or social. Merleau-Ponty's theory of the lived body offers us the best explanation for the significance of embodiment in human intelligence. Merleau-Ponty contends that humans have a lived body with which they relate to the world, and they are intelligent and reflective through that relationship. He argues that it is only a species of being that has a lived body that can be aware of the world and its contents. Thus, according to Merleau-Ponty, we can only be conscious of our experience of what is in the world as it appears to us insofar as we are in the world through our body, and insofar as we perceive what is in the world with our body.[96] In his theory of the lived body, one of the central aspects is perception phenomenologically conceived. What the lived body perceives (subject of perception) *presents itself with the world readymade* as the setting of every possible event. For Merleau-Ponty, perception is an event that forms a key component of human life in the world as an intelligent and reflective being.[97]

In Merleau-Ponty's theory, the body is not understood as a mere object, an inert mass, an extended external instrument. The body is thought of as a form of consciousness. Whatever we consider as mental states and activities like thinking, desire, belief etc. are bodily consciousness. Thus, Merleau-Ponty describes the body as a subjectivity.[98] With a body, we do not live in a world of representations but of experience, in a milieu in which there is no 'distinction or separation' by a gap between things and our own bodies. In this way, the body is understood as the envelope of our actions, and the ego (self)

---

[95] Danial Sonik and Alessandro Colarossi, *Becoming Artificial*, 27.

[96] Maurice Merleau-Ponty, *Phenomenology of Perception*, Colin Smith, trans. (New York: Routledge & Kegan Paul, 1958), 239.

[97] Danial Sonik and Alessandro Colarossi, *Becoming Artificial*, 28.

[98] Komarine Romdenh-Romluc, *Merleau-Ponty and Phenomenology of Perception* (London: Routledge, 2011), 62.

is the centre from which intentions radiate.[99] Merleau-Ponty gives the human body a unique understanding, quite a novelty to previous views in the history of thought. His theory characterises the body as both conscious reflexivity and corporeal reflex.[100]

The significance of Merleau-Ponty's theory of lived body is that it underscores a very crucial point that, no intelligence can be developed in a non-lived body framework. Thus, it is impossible to have disembodied intelligence as claimed in strong artificial intelligence. If we accept Merleau-Ponty's argument, then we find that the artefacts that 'embody' strong artificial intelligence lack the required perceptive interaction with the environment. What constitutes strong artificial intelligence is only a disembodied complex simulation, which cannot replicate perception that encompasses an inner subjective experience.[101] Otherwise, embodiment (lived body) is a key component in developing meaningful experiences of the physical and social environments through which intelligence is acquired. Otherwise, strong artificial intelligence is merely a sophistication of algorithms, which produces a simulated intelligence that can never replicate human intelligence because of its disembodiment. Human intelligence that is organic in nature and artificial intelligence that is simulated can never be equated.

Consciousness

What makes human intelligence inimitable by strong artificial intelligence is the former's possession of consciousness. Different experts in the philosophy of mind have defined and described consciousness, some of which can be adopted for *ad-hoc* use in this study. Thomas Nagel, for example, asserts that an organism is said to have consciousness if and only if it has an experience of something that

---

[99] Ted Toadvine and Leonard Lawlor, *The Merleau-Ponty Reader* (Illinois: Northwestern University Press), 8.

[100] M.C Dillon, *Merleau-Ponty's Ontology*, 2nd ed. (Indiana: Indiana University Press, 1988), 131.

[101] Danial Sonik and Alessandro Colarossi, *Becoming Artificial*, 30.

is like to be that organism.¹⁰² Thus, in Nagel's line of thought, the basic connotation of consciousness is the subjective experience of what it is like to be that subject. This has been termed as phenomenal consciousness i.e. experience that there is something "it is like" to be in that state. We can then assert that a conscious mental state is when there is experience of something it is like to be in that state.¹⁰³ Examples of conscious mental states include perceptual experience, sensation, mental imagery, emotional experience, occurrent thought, etc. In each of the states mentioned, there is a particular phenomenal characteristic of what it is like to be in that state e.g., there is something like to see as colour, to feel a very sharp pain, to feel a deep regret or joy, and to think that one is already for an activity.¹⁰⁴

There is a non-phenomenal notion of consciousness that Ned Block refers to as access consciousness and describes as something close to information processing image of phenomenal consciousness.¹⁰⁵ This non-phenomenal understanding of consciousness is computational in nature i.e., it has an information-processing character. There is yet another sense of understanding consciousness, commonly referred to as self-consciousness, which is, basically, the possession of the concept of the self and the capacity to use it in thinking about the self. In this way, self-consciousness can be described as a kind of "internal monitoring" of the phenomenal consciousness of one's self and consciousness of other states in which is self is.¹⁸ After a lengthy discussion about consciousness, we can now attempt to answer the question of whether artefacts such as computers and its sophistications can be conscious.

In trying to investigate if artefacts like computers that operate complex functions, can be conscious, it is important to note that, in the field of philosophy of mind, scholars have generally distinguished two

---

[102] Thomas Nagel, "What Is it like to Be a Bat?" in *Philosophy of Mind: Classical and Contemporary Readings*, David J. Chalmers ed., (New York: Oxford University Press, 2002), 212.

[103] David J. Chalmers, "Consciousness and Its Place in Nature" in *Philosophy of Mind: Classical and Contemporary Readings*, David J. Chalmers ed., (New York: Oxford University Press, 2002), 248.

[104] David J. Chalmers, "Consciousness and Its Place in Nature", 248.

[105] Ned Block, "The Concepts of Conscious" in in *Philosophy of Mind: Classical and Contemporary Readings*, David J. Chalmers ed., (New York: Oxford University Press, 2002), 208. [18] Ned Block, "The Concept of Conscious", 214.

approaches in the conception of the human mind. These approaches are neurobiological and computational. The first approach considers the biological nature of human experience as central in explaining the mind, whereas the second approach considers the mind (including consciousness) in terms of information processing, computation, and function in a system.[106] It is in the second approach to the understanding of the mind that the claim and project of strong artificial intelligence is based. Proponents of strong artificial intelligence think that the human mind can be replicated in artificial artefacts such as computers through complex simulations that perform information processing and computational functions. However, from the preceding discussion about consciousness, it is clear that consciousness is something beyond information processing and computation. It encompasses the two dimensions of understanding the mind, namely, the neurobiological and computational-functional dimensions, and transcends them to rise to the concept of the self that is referential in understanding consciousness.

We cannot talk of the concept of consciousness without the concept of the self. Selfhood lacks in artefacts such as computers and robots. Therefore, no amount of sophisticated simulation can replicate consciousness so long as it cannot invent selfhood. Self-consciousness understood as "internal monitoring" is akin to internal scanning in information processing. Indeed, computers perform internal self-scanning. However, we cannot think of them as conscious because their computational functioning lacks and can never possess selfhood.[107]

Intentionality

Another attribute of human intelligence that makes it inimitable by artificial intelligence is intentionality. Intentionality is the characteristic of the mental state by which it is directed at or about objects or states of affairs in the world.[108] Thus, mental states such as belief, desire and intention are intentional mental states because they

---

[106] Ned Block, "The Concept of Conscious", 214.

[107] Ned Block, "The Concept of Conscious", 214.

[108] John R. Searle, "Mind, Brains, and Programs" in *Introduction to Philosophy: Classical and Contemporary Readings"*, John Perry and Michael Bratman, eds. (New York: Oxford University Press, 1999), 380.

are directed at or about something or some state of affairs in the world. On the other hand, states such as undirected forms of anxiety, internal tranquility in a person, or depression, are not intentional states because they are not directed at some object or state of affairs.[109] Edmund Husserl is perhaps the best thinker whose thoughts about intentionality can be useful *ad-hoc* in this discussion. The concept of intentionality in Husserl is linked to lived experience and consciousness. The lived experiences are events that constitute conscious life. We can understand them in Husserl as passing subjective occurrences whose existence coincides with their being lived.[110]

Intentional lived experiences are characterised by directedness towards objects. Intentionality is therefore a kind of correlation between subjectivity and objectivity, which is a fundamental characteristic of consciousness.[111] The theory of intentionality in Husserl is different from that of the representation theory, which explains intentionality as a mere directedness towards an object in terms of mental representation that stands for external real object. In Husserl, it is an application of consciousness to such directedness. Thus, the three concepts in our discussion that are held to characterise human intelligence, namely, lived body (through which the subject lives an experience), consciousness, and intentionality are all related. Artificial intelligence cannot replicate human intelligence because these three named qualities of human intelligence cannot be simulated. In principle, suitably programmed computers can perform all that is produced by the computational procedure of the human mind. However, it is not the case that every activity of conscious intelligence is computational in nature, and not every such activity can be simulated.

Thus, the claim and assumption that artificial intelligence can develop an actual program that simulates the human mind in the entirety of its dimensions is an exercise in futility.

---

[109] John R. Searle, "Mind, Brains, and Programs", 380.

[110] Karl Weigelt, *The Signified Word: The Problem of Occasionality in Husserl's Phenomenology of Meaning* (Stockholm: Stockholm University, 2008), 84.

[111] Dermot Moran, *Edmund Husserl: Founder of Phenomenology* (London: Polity, 2005), 133.

Conclusion

This study appreciates the advancement in artificial intelligence technology that has improved many facets of human life to unprecedented levels. Today, we have improved health care due to accurate diagnosis, storage of the medical history of an individual, advanced surgical procedures, etc., thanks to artificial intelligence. We can now accurately arrive at any location without the struggle to sit down to spread a map for reading to find our location. We can order a taxi, food, purchases, and many other things on line, and do work from homes instead of going to the office or designated physical locations. Indeed, we can come up with a long list of how artificial intelligence has bettered our life. For this reason, this study compliments the employment of artificial intelligence as a tool in the hands of human beings in various ways for the purpose of improving human life. However, the study contests equating artificial intelligence to human intelligence, arguing that the two can only be analogized but can never be equated. Thus, the focus of the study is the refutation of the following arguments by the proponents of strong artificial intelligence: Firstly, that human intelligence can be replicated in artificial artefacts such that human intelligence and artificial intelligence can be held at par. Secondly, in the refutation of the main arguments of strong artificial intelligence, the study elaborates that human intelligence is different from artificial intelligence because it is an embodied, conscious, and intentional intelligence. All these three interconnected crucial attributes of human intelligence, namely, embodiment, consciousness, and intentionality are absent in artificial intelligence.

References:

ADLER, Block, Ned. "The Concepts of Conscious" in *Philosophy of Mind: Classical and Contemporary Readings*. David J. Chalmers, ed. New York: Oxford University Press, 2002.

CHALMERS, David J. "Consciousness and Its Place in Nature" in *Philosophy of Mind: Classical and Contemporary Readings*. David J. Chalmers, ed. New York: Oxford University Press, 2002.

DILLON, M.C. *Merleau-Ponty's Ontology*, 2nd ed. Indiana: Indiana University Press, 1988).

LOCKE, John. "Psychological Properties Define the Self" in *Introduction to Philosophy: Classical and Contemporary Readings*. Louis P. Pojman, edit. New York: Oxford University Press, 2004.

MERLEAU-PONTY, Maurice. *Phenomenology of Perception*, Colin Smith, trans. New York: Routledge & Kegan Paul, 1958.

MORAN, Dermot. *Edmund Husserl: Founder of Phenomenology*. London: Polity, 2005.

NAGEL, Thomas. "What Is it like to Be a Bat?" in *Philosophy of Mind: Classical and Contemporary Readings*, David J. Chalmers ed. New York: Oxford University Press, 2002.

ROMDENH-ROMLUC, Komarine. *Merleau-Ponty and Phenomenology of Perception*. London: Routledge, 2011.

SEARLE, John R. "Can Computers Think?" in *Philosophy of Mind: Classical and Contemporary Readings*, David J. Chalmers ed. New York: Oxford University Press, 2002.

_____, "Minds, Brains and Programs", Behavioural and Brain Sciences", in *Philosophy of Mind: Contemporary Readings*, Timothy O'Connor and David Robb, eds. New York: Routledge, 1999.

SHANAHAN, Murray. *The Technological Singularity*. Massachusetts: MIT Press, 2015.

SONIK, Danial and Alessandro Colarossi. *Becoming Artificial: A Philosophical Exploration into Artificial Intelligence and What It means to be Human*. London: Imprint Academic Ltd, 2020.

TOADVINE, Ted and Leonard Lawlor. *The Merleau-Ponty Reader*. Illinois: North Western University Press, 2007.

WEIGELT, Karl. *The Signified Word: The Problem of Occasionality in Husserl's Phenomenology of Meaning*. Stockholm: Stockholm University, 2008.

PART THREE

AI AND THE MORAL QUESTIONS

AI and Free Will
Critical Perspectives Based on Saint Thomas Aquinas' Concept of *Liberum Arbitrium*

Alagbe Domara, Bernard Domara Alagbe (MCCJ), holds a PhD in Philosophy, with a focus on Political Philosophy. He is, currently, Lecturer at Tangaza University's Institute of Philosophy, and Apostles of Jesus Institute of Philosophy and Theology (AJIPT), Nairobi – Kenya.

Abstract

This article examines Saint Thomas Aquinas' concept of "Liberum Arbitrium" (free will) in relation with artificial intelligence (AI). With the current developments of AI (Humanoid Robot and Reinforcement Learning Agent for instance), the philosophical question about free will for intelligent machines, acting like humans, has become more relevant. If for Saint Thomas Aquinas, human acts are embedded in the intellect i.e., knowledge and judgment, and "Liberum Arbitrium" which is the power to choose among alternatives, consequently, can machines have free will by the fact that they are intelligent and can act like humans? Is only the power of choosing consequently and sequentially the ultimate expression of free will? Our critical perspectives will examine the computational theory of mind in its essential aspect of cognition, which Saint Thomas Aquinas also relates to the free will. The researcher analyses the automaton theory, which is based on a deterministic framework, challenging the possibility of free will; and lastly take into consideration the process of deliberation, the intentionality of the act, and the ultimate end of the free act.

Key Words: Liberum Arbitrium, Free will, Artificial Intelligence, Computation, Automaton.

Introduction

In his article entitled "Free Will – even for Robots", John McCarthy concluded by stating: "AI needs a more developed formal theory of free will, i.e., the structure of choice a robot can have and what it can usefully know about it."[112] In McCarthy's statement, we can identify two characteristics of what seems to be free will for AI: the capacity to choose and the awareness of the choice like humans. Therefore, can AI have free will? This question is similar to the one asked by Alan Turing fifty years earlier "Can machines think?"[113] That allowed him to explore the capacities of the so-called "intelligent machines" to compete with humans in the cognitive process of acquiring and applying intelligence in various areas of human activities. In fact, these two perspectives lead to the underlying question about AI: "can machines act as humans do indistinguishably?"

However, Human acts, according to Saint Thomas Aquinas, are embedded in the intellect (knowledge and judgement) and the *Liberum Arbitrium* which is free will.[114] Consequently, can machines have free will by the fact that they are intelligent and can perform some tasks as humans do? Can their performance be understood according to the structure of human acts and the cognitive processes of acquiring knowledge and understanding?

Our perspective will be a critical analysis of the possibility to attribute the *free will* to AI, based on Saint Thomas Aquinas' concept of *Liberum Arbitrium*. Assuming his conception, we shall discuss two main theories such as the computational theory of mind in its essential aspects of cognition, to which saint Thomas Aquinas relates the free will, and the automaton theory, based on a deterministic framework. This critical perspective will end up by analysing the intentionality and the ultimate end of the "presumed free acts" of intelligent machines.

---

[112] John McCarthy, "Free Will even for Robots", *Journal of Experimental and Theoretical Artificial Intelligence*, no. 12 (Mars 2000): 341-342.

[113] Alan Turing, "Computing and machinery intelligence", *Mind. A quarterly Review of Psychology and Philosophy* LIX, no. 236 (October 1950): 433-460.

[114] Saint Thomas Aquinas, *Summa Theologica (STh.)*, I, q. 82-83.

Saint Thomas Aquinas' Concept of Liberum Arbitrium and Its Relation to AI

Free will is generally understood like the power of acting without the constraint of necessity or fate. It is the freedom of the will. As a philosophical problem, free will has always been about whether humans have free will or not; whether free will pertains to the animal or inanimate objects (like a stone for instance). The same question is moving towards the so-called intelligent machines. The question seems to be irrelevant as far as Saint Thomas Aquinas is concerned, since for him it is evident that the inanimate realities don't have free will, because they lack judgement and knowledge. Can the same consideration be made for intelligent machines that are equipped with the capacity to "judge" and to "know", because rightly they are "intelligent." In this perspective, it is so important to understand saint Thomas Aquinas' concept of free will.

Saint Thomas Aquinas' Concept of Free Will

Liberum Arbitrium, which is "free judgment," according to Saint Thomas, "in its strict sense denotes an act, in the common manner of speaking we call free will, that which is the principle of the act by which man judges freely."[115] Hence, Saint Thomas Aquinas distinguishes two understandings of freedom of the will. Freedom of the will, according to the broad conception i.e., *Libertas Voluntatis*, "requires sourcehood but not alternative possibilities"; that is the source of the act is the agent's will. In a narrow conception, freedom of the will, which is *Liberum Arbitrium*, "requires alternative possibilities in addition to the sourcehood."[116] So, free will is both an act and the principle of the act. On the one hand, by act, free will is the power to choose among alternatives. On the other hand, the principle of the act is about the will that moves the agent to act. However, Saint Thomas Aquinas stresses more on the narrow conception of free will by asserting that "the proper act of free will is choice: for we say that we have free will, because we can take one thing while refusing another; and it is to choose. Therefore,

---

[115] Saint Thomas Aquinas, *Summa Theologica*, I, q. 83, a. 2.
[116] Tobbias Hoffman – Cyrille Michon, "Aquinas on free will and intellectual determinism", *Philosopher's Imprint*, Vol XVII, no. 17 (May 2017): 1-36, 3.

we can consider the nature of free will by considering the nature of choice."[117] From this perspective, taking into consideration the two conceptions, we can argue that free will is the ability to choose, based on a free judgment done by a free agent. Therefore, it is fitting at this point to analyse the "ability" to choose and the nature of the judgment.

Free will is the power or the ability of the agent to choose freely and efficaciously within choice situations. To deepen our understanding of free will, it is important to apprehend the concept of power and ability. Power or ability has to be defined in terms of "can". However, Peter van Inwagen, considering the power and ability in terms of "can" determines five perspectives that the power or ability (can) of an agent to act is not. It is not firstly about "moral or legal permissibility" whereby the agent is allowed by a competent authority or by moral law to act. Moreover, for saint Thomas Aquinas, free will does not primarily imply moral responsibility; moral responsibility is just incidental in the act of choosing: "But free will is indifferent to good and evil choice."[118] Free will, afterwards, it is neither a "physical power", nor an "epistemic power", a "causal power or capacity", it is neither about "skill or accomplishment"[119]. It is, in saint Thomas Aquinas' view, the concurrence of an "apprehensive power" and an "appetitive power."[120]

Actually, the adjective "apprehensive" is from classical Latin *apprehensio* (from the verb *apprehendere*), that is the act of "capturing with the mind", which means the ability to comprehend, to understand fully. Therefore, the "apprehensive power" is the ability to understand; it is the power of the mind to understand and to judge "that something should be avoided and sought."[121] There resides free will as the power to choose. Consequently, free will is the apprehensive power on which the choice is based. It is not a moral or legal permissibility, nor a physical power, nor an epistemic power, nor a causal power, nor about skills. It is the power of the mind to understand and judge fully whereby the choice can be made. The choice indeed involves not only the apprehensive power, but also the appetitive power. In a choice, there is

---

[117] *STh*, I, q. 83, a. 3.

[118] Ibid., I, q. 83, a. 2.

[119] Van Inwagen Peter, *An Essay on free will*, Oxford: Clarendon Press, 1983, 9-12.

[120] *STh*, I, q. 83, a. 1.

[121] Ibid., I, q. 83, a. 1.

the concurrence of the cognitive power and appetitive powers. In this perspective, cognitive power requires counsel by which we judge one thing to be preferred to another. Thence, the appetitive power should accept the judgment of the counsel. Thus, free will is also an appetitive power that accompanies the apprehensive power. This concurrence shows the relation between the will and the intellect in choosing.

The intellect, according to Saint Thomas, may be understood in two ways: on the one hand, the intellect is the ability to apprehend the universal being and truth; on the other hand, it is the particular power of having a determinate act. The will as the appetite for universal good, is a determinate power of the soul having a determinate act. These two powers include one another in their act, because the intellect understands that the will wills and the will wills the intellect to understand.[122] It should be noted that Saint Thomas Aquinas' concept of free will is not a deterministic perspective and does not imply intellectual determinism.

Humans have free will because they are rational: they judge by their apprehensive power that something should be avoided or sought. Reason is characteristic of human beings. Free will therefore is a specific character of reason, the distinctive trait of man.

Saint Thomas Aquinas' concept of free will can be summarized in four essential elements:

- Free will is the power to choose among alternatives: "But to choose is to desire something for the sake of obtaining something else: wherefore, properly speaking, it regards the means to the end."[123] Accordingly, free will is part of a strategical and teleological framework. It is then the capacity to act intentionally.
- Moreover, the power in question is apprehensive and appetitive in the sense that there is concurrence between the intellect and the will, in order to choose. The free choice is based on the cognitive processes of willing, understanding, and judging.
- By their apprehensive power, humans judge freely and choose their actions and apply knowledge to what they do. This implies

---

[122] *STh*, q. 82, a. 4.
[123] *STh*, q. 86, a. 4.

an awareness of their actions. That awareness or consciousness is a certain pronouncement of the mind.
- Man has free will, that is, the power to choose by the fact that they are rational. The rationality underlines their capacity to argue, to compute and to represent reality.

Thomas Aquinas' perspective hence offers the possibility to confront critically the hypothesis of free will in AI.

AI and Free Will

Artificial Intelligence (AI) is the possession of intelligence or the exercise of thoughts by machines. AI is a computational technique that makes machines behave intelligently like humans. This computational technique empowers the machines to learn and make their own decision without relying on people to tell them what to do and how to react. Therefore, a machine is considered to be intelligent under these conditions: "if it can analyse information and extract insights beyond the obvious"; if it "can learn and make their own decision"[124]. Empowered in such a way, they can perform some complicated tasks like playing chess better than humans. Specifically, Artificial Intelligence is subdivided in three types: machine learning – deep learning, soft computing, and computational intelligence. For instance, "machine learning is the use of data and statistics to create intelligent machines".[125] Its characteristic is the mimicry of human intelligence, the use of neural networks with many layers in order to imitate the structure of the human brain.[126] The soft computing on its hand, is used "to bring precision to issues such as linguistic variables." Finally, "the computational intelligence uses group intelligence observed in nature to build intelligent machines." It so appears that intelligence is the main dimension of these artefacts. Moreover, intelligence is the essential characteristic of rationality. It refers to the cognitive process of understanding, judging, and making decisions. So, we presume that a learning machine for instance, being intelligent, is rational. If free will

---

[124] Tshilidji Marwala, *Rational machines and artificial intelligence*, London, Academic Press Elsevier Inc 2021, 6.
[125] Ibid.
[126] Ibid.

is embedded, according to Saint Thomas in the intellect and in human rationality, it may be concluded that AI has free will, by the very fact that it is a rational agent, able to make decisions and to choose among alternatives.

By the fact that learning machines are intelligent, they are engaged in deliberative behaviours, confronting options and choosing among alternatives (when Alpha Zotero plays the game of chess for example). Secondly, the process of choosing is based on the cognitive processes where the intellect and the will are enforced on the act of choosing. AI also seems to be based on human cognitive processes of determining the right choice to make. If the power of choosing is an apprehensive and appetitive power, AI seems to follow the processes of the mind and makes decision about what can be avoided or sought. These similarities between a rational agent like AI and a human being call for a critical understanding of the claim to attribute free will to AI.

The first claim is from the computational theory or functionalism which sustains with Alan Turing and John McCarthy that the mind is a computational system, therefore uploading it in a machine, it will behave like humans about deliberation, decision-making and problem-resolution. Hence, we shall take into consideration the computational theory of mind inasmuch free will pertains to reason, understood as the capacity to compute, to argue and to represent reality.

Functionalism or Computational Theory of Mind and Free Will

The computational theory of mind (CTM) defends the perspective that the mind is a "special kind of computer:" a computational system. It has become a claim for strong AI which is an AI with "mental capabilities and functions that mimic human brain." In that sense, "the computer is not merely a tool in the study of the mind; rather, the appropriately programmed computer really is a mind, in the sense that computers given the right programs can be literally said to understand and have other cognitive states."[127] To such a kind of

---

[127] John Searl, "Minds, brains and programs", *The behavioral and brain sciences*, no 3 (September 1980): 417-457, 417.

machine, should be given subjective conscious experience and a mind. In addition, the CTM sustains that cognition, conscious and neural activity are a form of computation. This conviction leads to think that uploading human mind in a robot would make the robot exactly behave like a human being.

The exponents of this theory have been influenced by Alan Turing who with his so-known "Turing test" and "Turing machines", explored the capabilities of digital computers to behave like humans do. Moreover, the progress in Computer science has led to AI whose aim is no longer to build computing machines but to construct machines able to execute mental tasks like reasoning, decision-making, and problem-solving. On the other hand, based on these core mental tasks, John McCarthy supports that strong AI would have free will as humans have. Pointing out the difference between "having choices and being conscious of these choices,"[128] McCarthy emphasizes that both are important even for robots because they characterize a free agent.

The computational theory of mind led to the claim of free will for strong AI. Nevertheless, the mind refers to the part of the human person that thinks, feels, perceives, and judges: it is the intellective and appetitive part of the human being. It can also be understood as the ability to think, to reason, and to remember. It also refers to consciousness, that is, the ability to be aware of things and of one's actions. Therefore, AI claims to have these attributes by the fact that it "simulates" the human mind and human cognitive processes. The conception of will as an intellectual power highlights the role of cognitive processes in willing and choosing. In that perspective, the rapport between free will and mind can easily be perceived.

Our critical perspectives, discussing the hypothesis of the strong AI with Saint Thomas Aquinas, will point out three problematics, namely, reason (by which cognitive processes are triggered), the power to choose, and conscience. In other words, we shall investigate whether strong AI has free will by the fact that it is a rational agent, able to choose among alternatives, and aware of its choices.

---

[128] John McCarthy, "Free will even for robots", *Journal of experimental and theoretical Artificial Intelligence*, no. 12 (Mars 2000): 341.

Human Rational Agency, Artificial Rational Agency, and Free Will

Saint Thomas Aquinas clearly states that humans have free will because they are rational. Human rationality implies three dimensions, namely the computation, the argumentation, and the representation.

Regarding computation, physical systems empowered with AI are computing devices, able to compute in minute what Human mind cannot. Reason as computation also implies the evaluation of the profit and loss in action to perform in order to choose the best. Thus, computation is about a strategical action in order to achieve a particular goal. In this, the strategic perspective of computation is used in Defence Research for instance. Although AI can compute and perform strategic action in order to achieve goals, is this enough evidence to attribute free will to AI?

The argumentative dimension of rationality refers to dialogue, cooperation, negotiation, and deliberation. Hence, argumentation involves interaction, it is not just about the "reasoning in the recesses of single minds."[129] It is about intelligent interaction and logical rigour. In this perspective, AI is empowered to have intelligent interaction with its environment and is based on a rigorous formal logic, which allows AI to understand and interpret the input: it is, for instance, equipped with the semantics of logic programs, persuasive medical diagnostic systems, negotiation dialogues in multi-agent systems. But can the argumentative dimension in AI be a condition of the possession of free will?

The representation is human ability to access external reality through symbols or abstraction. It is about how human brain represents the reality in order to understand it and to adapt itself accordingly. It is about performing intelligence behaviour which is associated to the existence of applicable knowledge. The applicable knowledge is acquired and stored through perception, learning, reasoning and planning. In AI, there is knowledge representation system (KKR: Knowledge Representation and Reasoning), able to provide due information about the external reality so that AI may be able to take information from its environment through listening, seeing, and

---

[129] Johan van Benthem, Foreword to Iyad Rahwan – Guillermo R. Simari (ed.), *Argumentation in Artificial Intelligence*, Springer Science + Business Media LLC, New York 2009, vii.

reading; it can also through deep learning algorithm study, learn and remember (memory). It can use what it has learned to plan and perform actions. But is the representation of knowledge convincing for the possession of free?

Analysing these three dimensions of rationality in AI, it is undeniable that AI is a rational Agent. But from rationality to free will in AI, some considerations should be made.

Firstly, a human being is rational by nature, wherefore he has free will. It underscores that free will is the power of reason which is the essence of man as the "Imago Dei". Secondly, the will, as an appetite, is the power of the soul by which humans are inclined towards something. The soul is immortal, immaterial, and a spiritual form, a principle for knowledge. Thirdly, the cognitive processes of acquiring and applying knowledge need a biological substrate which is the brain. Therefore, it is not enough to simulate the human brain's cognitive processes in an artefact and claim to have free will. Free will is the proper attribute of reason by the fact that reason is the essence of human beings, and the will is the power of the soul. On the contrary, AI is rational by simulation or by mimicry not by nature. Consequently, the rationality in AI cannot imply free will.

The Power to Choose

According to Saint Thomas Aquinas, the proper act of free will is choice: "For we say that we have free will because we can take one thing while refusing another; and this is to choose. Therefore, we must consider the nature of free will by considering the nature of choice."[130] Thus, it is so important to analyse the nature of choice that AI can make. Actually, a choice according to Aristotle is a desire proceeding from counsel. For Saint Thomas Aquinas, a free choice needs the collaboration between the cognitive power and the appetitive power. In a choice for instance, counsel is required by which we judge one thing to be preferred to another. At the same time, the appetitive power should accept the judgement of the counsel. Moreover, the proper object of choice is the means to the end. Considering the nature of choice, it would be interesting to analyse the choice in AI.

---

[130] *STh*, I, q. 83, a. 3.

AI is empowered to make choices, based on the programming system. At the same time, it is difficult to understand how the cognitive power relates to the appetitive power in AI in order to perform chosen actions; how the appetitive power accompanies the apprehensive power, given that they are powers of the soul. Moreover, to choose, according to Saint Thomas Aquinas is "to desire something for the sake of obtaining something else: properly speaking, it regards the means to the end."[131] Human beings as intellectual or rational beings seek goodness through their free choices. Human choices as desire aim at the universal goodness. If the nature of the free choice is to be the means to an end which is goodness, that is God, according to Saint Thomas Aquinas, it is, therefore, difficult to assert that AI has free will by the fact that it can just choose freely among alternatives. How can a system of algorithms seek God in its choices? AI cannot be said to have free will just by the mere fact that it can choose among alternatives. Moreover, the awareness of one's choice is characteristic of that same power of choosing, that is related to free will.

Consciousness in Humans and AI

The CTM holds that consciousness should be attributed to AI. Consciousness is the state of being able through the senses and mental power to grasp one's surrounding and what's going on in it. In this section, we shall consider the dimension of awareness that we relate to Saint Thomas Aquinas' conception of conscience. According to Aquinas, conscience is a certain "pronouncement of the mind." It is the application of knowledge to something. "For conscience, according to the very nature of the world, implies relation of knowledge to something: For conscience, may be resolved into *cum alio scientia*, i.e., knowledge applied to an individual case."[132] It is undeniable, from this conception that AI establishes relation between knowledge and things. But the nature of this relation will make the difference between humans and AI. For Saint Thomas, conscience is an act and is said "to witness, to bind or incite, or also accuse, torment or rebuke. And all these follow the application of knowledge, or science to what we do."[133] If we

---

[131] STh, q. 83, a. 4.
[132] *STh*, q. 79, a. 11.
[133] *STh*, q. 79, a. 11.

consider the hypothesis that conscience should be given to AI, how can it witness, bind, incite, accuse, torment or rebuke?

In Saint Thomas Aquinas' perspective, there are three ways by which conscience as an act is related to what we do: by witnessing, we recognize that we have done or not done something; by binding, we acknowledge that something should be done or not done and by judging, we know that something is well done or poorly done. Analysing the intelligent behaviour of a deep learning machine, such as a reinforcement learning agent, which is able to learn from experience and adapt itself in the new future contexts based on what it has learned, it is probable to say that AI has consciousness, that is, the awareness of what is happening and the relation of knowledge to something. But conscience implies imputability as assumption of one's free choices. In that, the defenders of the consciousness failed to impute AI.

The claims of the computational theory of mind are unsupported by Thomas Aquinas' conception of free will as a rational power for the above reasons. This leads us to analyse the hypothesis of free will in AI from the automaton theory.

Automation Theory and Free Will

In AI, an automaton system empowers a device with a predetermined sequence of operations automatically. It is a system whose operation is based on a deterministic framework. In this perspective, the relation between free will and the automaton can be analysed from Saint Thomas Aquinas' conception of the relation between the will and necessity. Before analysing the rapport between necessity and the will in the light of the deterministic framework of AI, it is important to notice that Saint Thomas Aquinas' conception of free will is non-deterministic; but the will has a natural necessity following its nature.

The will considered as the principle of an action, has a natural necessity that inclines towards universal goodness. Thence, there are two necessities: internal and external. By internal necessity, the will follows reason, inasmuch to will something, that thing must be known. The external necessity, namely the maker of will (God), according to Saint Thomas Aquinas, causes to move. This external agent is not opposed to the natural inclination of the will which is towards the universal goodness. In this, the will is free and is never under coercion.

Apparently, the automaton system follows a kind of necessity by the fact that the automaton device automatically moves according to its internal structure, which is its proper setting. In this perspective, the deterministic framework understood as an internal necessity of the automaton device, should not be opposed to free will. However, as said above, the necessity by nature derives from reason which is the essence of human beings. In an AI device equipped with an automaton system, the necessity is not by nature but by mimicry and programming. In this perspective, the automaton theory in relation to natural necessity in humans cannot guarantee the possibility of free will.

Intentionality, Ultimate End, Free Will and AI

Human choices and acts are motivated and intentionally oriented toward an end. The free choice is the means to an end, which is the universal goodness. Directly and indirectly, human acts aim at an ultimate end which is happiness, that is, to know and to love God, insofar as Saint Thomas Aquinas is concerned. Therefore, human beings do not act for the sake of acting. The intentionality as tension towards something can be contemplated in AI but cannot be contemplated as tension towards a universal goodness which is God; it can neither be contemplated as tension towards the ultimate end-happiness, which consists in knowing and loving God. Hence, free will in relation to motivation, intentionality and ultimate end is difficult to determine in AI.

Conclusion

The analysis of the claims of free will for AI, from Saint Thomas Aquinas' concept of *Liberum Arbitrium*, led us to take into consideration the CTM, the automaton theory and the intentionality. The outcome of our critical perspective is that the claims of free will are unsupported in saint Thomas Aquinas' conception of *Liberum Arbitrium* for these reasons:

ISSUES IN ARTIFICIAL INTELLIGENCE:
A PHILOSOPHICAL INTERROGATION

Man has free will because he is a rational being by nature. AI is a rational agent by simulation of human rationality. Moreover, the will is the power of the soul; not the power of the combination of algorithms. The cognitive processes need a biological substrate, i.e., the brain, which is lacking in AI.

The will is free by its proper nature, following its natural inclination towards goodness and the ultimate end. Although it follows its natural inclination, it is never under coercion. On the contrary, AI in the perspective of the automaton system inclines in a deterministic manner, to its particular end according to its setting, but never naturally.

The choice is a means to an end, not an end in itself. It is therefore obvious that humans do not act for the sake of acting, but for the sake of an end that AI cannot conceive.

The consciousness in a human act is more than learning from experience. Applying knowledge to something or being aware of one's act implies the ability to witness, to bind, and to judge. Thence, AI cannot be bound to its own acts, although it can choose among alternatives.

The question of free will in AI is complex and nuanced, carrying the inherent risk for those contemplating it to succumb to the temptation of assessing AI through a human lens. We aspire to have avoided such a snare. Nevertheless, AI represents a challenge to humanity urging us to delve into a deeper understanding of our identity in order to fully grasp the nature of AI.

References:

BRACHMAN, Ronald J., and LEVESQUE, Hector J., eds. *Knowledge Representation and Reasoning*. San Francisco: Elsevier 2004.

DREYFUS, Hubert L. *What Computers Can't Do? Of artificial intelligence*. New York: Harper & Row, 1972.

HOFFMAN, Tobbias, and MICHON Cyrille. "Aquinas on Free Will and Intellectual Determinism". *Philosopher's Imprint* XVII, no. 17 (May 2017): 1-36.

INWAGEN, Van Peter. *An Essay on Free Will*. Oxford: Clarendon Press, 1983.

MARWALA, Tshilidji. *Rational Machines and Artificial Intelligence*. London: Academic Press Elsevier Inc, 2021.

MCCARTHY, John. "Free Will even for Robots". *Journal of Experimental and Theoretical Artificial Intelligence*, no. 12 (Mars 2000): 341-352.

MCLAUGHlin, Brian P., and COHEN, Jonathan, eds. *Contemporary Debates in Philosophy of Mind*. Malden: Blackwell, 2007.

RAHWAN, Iyad, and GUILLERMO R. Simari, ed. *Argumentation in Artificial Intelligence*. New York: Springer Science + Business Media LLC, 2009.

RICH, Elaine. *Automata, Computability and Complexity: Theory and applications*. New Jersey: Prentice Hall 2019.

SAINT THOMAS AQUINAS, *Summa Theologica*, I, q. 79-83.

SEARL, John. "Minds, brains and programs". *The Behavioral and Brain Sciences*, no 3 (September 1980): 417-457.

TURING, Alan. "Computing and Machinery Intelligence". *Mind. A quarterly Review of Psychology and Philosophy* LIX, no. 236 (October 1950): 433-460.

An Evaluation of the Philosophy of Artificial Intelligence (AI) Through the Lens of Kantian Notion of Freewill

Nyaga Anastasio holds a master's degree in philosophy, and is, currently a PhD student at The Catholic University of Eastern Africa (CUEA), Nairobi. He teaches Philosophy at the Institute of Philosophy (IOP) and at the School of Art and Social Sciences (SASS), both in Tangaza University, Nairobi - Kenya, and also at the Apostles of Jesus Institute of Philosophy and Theology (AJIPT), Nairobi – Kenya.

Abstract

The question of Artificial Intelligence (AI) is not as recent as it seems to be popularized by the current technological epochs. The history of AI dates back to classical antiquity period (8th century BCE – 5th century CE) with mythical stories and rumours of artificial creatures endowed with intelligence or consciousness by master craftsmen. Consequently, the seeds of modern AI can be said to have been planted by philosophers who attempted to describe the process of human thinking as the mechanical manipulation of symbols. With the advent of programmable computers in 1940s, we see a paradigm shift from pure human thinking to machine based mathematical reasoning. The philosophy of AI therefore, can be termed as a branch of philosophy of mind and philosophy of computer science which explores AI and its implications for knowledge and understanding of intelligence, ethics, consciousness, epistemology and free will.

It is therefore, the attempt of this article to evaluate the philosophy of AI through the lens of Kantian notion of freewill. In so doing, the article will explore the key aspects of Kantian philosophy, particularly his ideas about autonomy, rationality, and moral agency. Kant's philosophy lays great emphasis on human autonomy and the moral responsibility that arises from the exercise of free will. Applying these concepts to AI raises important questions about the nature of AI, its autonomy, and the ethical implications of its actions.

Key Words: Kant, Freewill, Human Autonomy, Artificial Intelligence (AI), Philosophy of AI.

Introduction

The story of Artificial Intelligence (AI) – if I may call it a story – is not as recent as it apparently appears to be popularized by the current technological era. The AI's history dates back to classical antiquity period (8th century BCE – 5th century CE) with mythical stories and rumors of artificial creatures endowed with intelligence or consciousness by master craftsmen.[134] We also read some medieval legends of artificial beings. For instance, in his book *Of the Nature of Things*, the Swiss alchemist, Paracelsus, describes a procedure that he claims can fabricate an "artificial man". By placing the "sperm of a man" in horse dung and feeding it the "Arcanum of Mans blood" after 40 days, the concoction will become a living infant.[135]

Although historians trace the idea of 'automata'[136] to the Middle Ages – when the first self-moving devices were invented – the concepts of artificial, lifelike creatures' dates back to the myths and legends from at least about 2,700 years ago in the ancient Greece. Adrienne Mayor, in his book *God's and Robots: Myths, Machines and Ancient Dreams of Technology,* says, "long before technological advances made self-moving devise possible, ideas about creating artificial life and robots

---

[134] Apollonious Rhodious, *The Argonautika: Expanded Edition*, (California: University of California Press, 2007), 355.

[135] Stanton J. Linden, The Alchemy Reader: From Hermes Trismegistus to Isaac Newton (New York: Cambridge University), 2003, 18.

[136] Automatons are abstract models of machines that perform computations on an input by moving through a series of states or configurations. At each state of the computation, a transition function determines the next configuration on the basis of a finite portion of the present configuration.

were explored in ancient Greek myths."[137] Needlessly to say, this book reveals how some of today's most advanced innovations in robotics and AI were foreshadowed in ancient Greek mythologies. Indeed, this shows how science has always been driven by human imagination.

From the philosophical panorama, the seeds of modern AI can be said to have been planted by philosophers who attempted to describe the process of human thinking as the mechanical manipulation of symbols. With the advent of programmable computers in 1940s, we see a paradigm shift from pure human thinking to machine based mathematical reasoning. From a general perspective therefore, the philosophy of AI can be termed as a branch of philosophy of mind and philosophy of computer science which explores AI and its implications for knowledge and understanding of intelligence, ethics, consciousness, epistemology and free will.

It is therefore, the attempt of this article to evaluate the philosophy of AI through the lens of Kantian notion of freewill. In so doing, the paper will explore the key aspects of Kantian philosophy, particularly his ideas about autonomy, rationality, and moral agent, relating these aspects to AI. Kant's philosophy lays great emphasis on human autonomy and the moral responsibility that arises from the exercise of free will. Interrogating the philosophy of AI vis-a-vis Kantian notion of freewill raises profound ethical questions with regard to moral responsibility of the agent.

Meaning and Evolution of Artificial Intelligence

Artificial Intelligence (AI), sometimes called "machine intelligence," is a type of intelligence demonstrated by machines, in contrast to the natural intelligence displayed by humans and other animals, such as learning and problem solving. AI can also be defined as the study of computer systems that attempt to model and apply the intelligence of the human mind. Researchers in AI are concerned with the study of "intelligent agents," any device that perceives its environment and takes actions that maximizes its chance of successfully

---

[137] Adrienne Mayor, *God's and Robots: Myths, Machines and Ancient Dreams of Technology* (New York: Princeton University Press, 2018), 206.

achieving its appropriated tasks.[138] AI encompasses a wide range of techniques and approaches, including machine learning, natural language processing, robotics, and cognitive computing.

While science limitedly portrays AI as robots with human-like characteristics, AI can encompass anything from Google's search algorithms to IBM's Watson, to autonomous weapons. Alan Turing has been termed as among the pioneer research to carry out s substantial study in the field of machine intelligence,[139] but the term 'artificial intelligence' itself was introduced by John McCarthy[140] in 1956 during a workshop that saw the formal inception of AI as an academic discipline. Alan Turing's seminal paper "Computing Machinery and Intelligence" in 1950 introduced the concept of the Turing Test as a measure of machine intelligence.[141] Consequently, the Logic Theorist, developed by Allen Newell and Herbert A. Simon in 1955, was one of the first AI programs, demonstrating that machines could perform tasks that required human-like reasoning. Three years later, John McCarthy developed the Lisp programming language – one of the oldest high-level programming language known for its simple syntax based on parenthesized expressions – which became the primary language for AI research and symbolic computation.[142]

In recent times, the advent of deep learning[143] revolutionized AI, leading to breakthroughs in areas like natural language processing, autonomous driving, and medical diagnostics. AI systems like Google's AlphaGo, which defeated the world champion Go player in 2016, and Open AI's GPT-3, a state-of-the-art language model, have showcased

---

[138] Russell, Stuart J., and Peter Norvig, *Artificial Intelligence: A Modern Approach*. 3rd ed., Prentice Hall, 2010), 1-2.

[139] Jack Copeland, (Ed.) The Essential Turing: The Ideas that gave Birth to the Computer Age. Oxford: Clarendon Press, 2004), 27.

[140] Chatterjee et al., "Evolution of Artificial Intelligence and Its Impact on Human Rights: From Sociolegal Perspective," International Journal of Law and Management, 62(2): January, 2021, 184-205.

[141] Alan Turing, "Computing Machinery and Intelligence." *Mind*, vol. 59, no. 236, 1950. 433-460.

[142] John McCarthy, "Programs with Common Sense. *Teddington Conference on the Mechanization of Thought Processes*, 1958, pp. 75-91.

[143] Deep learning involves the use of neural networks with many layers (hence "deep" learning) to model complex patterns in data.

the potential of AI in tackling complex tasks.[144] As a whole, recent developments in AI have been marked by significant advancements across various domains, driven largely by breakthroughs in machine learning, neural networks, and computational capabilities.

Artificial Intelligence (AI) can be broadly categorized into two types: Strong AI and Weak AI. These distinctions help clarify the different capabilities and objectives of AI systems. Strong AI, also known as General AI or Artificial General Intelligence (AGI), refers to AI systems with the capability to understand, learn, and apply intelligence across a wide range of tasks, similar to human cognitive abilities. These systems would possess consciousness, self-awareness, and genuine understanding. However, scholars have argued that true Strong AI does not yet exist and remains a theoretical goal.[145]

Weak AI, also known as Narrow AI, refers to AI systems designed and trained for a specific task or a narrow range of tasks. These systems do not possess consciousness, self-awareness, or genuine understanding. They excel at particular functions but lack general intelligence. They include **voice assistants** such as Siri, Alexa, and Google Assistant that can perform tasks like setting reminders, playing music, and answering questions but cannot understand context beyond their programmed capabilities. Recommendation systems like Netflix and Amazon use AI to suggest movies and products based on user preferences and behavior, but these systems do not understand the content itself.[146] Finally, we also have **autonomous vehicles**, for instance, self-driving cars that can navigate and make driving decisions based on sensor data and algorithms, but they lack broader cognitive abilities.[147]

---

[144] Nilsson Nils, *The Quest for Artificial Intelligence*, (Cambridge University Press, 2010) 267-268.

[145] Stuart Russell and Peter Norvig, *Artificial Intelligence: Modern Approach*, Third Edition (Ithaca: Cornel University, 2011) 935-937.

[146] Clair Brown & Greg Linden, "Two Decades of Recommender Systems at Amazon.com." *IEEE Internet Computing*, 21(3), (2017). 12-18.

[147] Todd Litman, *Autonomous Vehicle Implementation Predictions Implications for Transport Planning*, (Victoria Transport Policy Institute, 2020) 3.

How intelligent is Artificial Intelligence?

Is AI really intelligent? This is seemingly a very utopia question that this article may not claim to interrogate at this moment. Perhaps, we would have started by asking what we mean by intelligence. What is intelligence? A short question, but needing a discursive response. In the first place, we must contingently acknowledge that the definition of 'intelligence' is one of the unsolved problems in philosophy. Etymologically, the word intelligence is derived from two Latin nouns, *intellegentia* and *intellectus*, which in turn stem from the verb *intelligere*, meaning to comprehend or perceive. In the Middle Ages, the word *intellectus* (latin) became the scholarly technical term for understanding and a translation for the Greek philosophical term *nous*. *Nous* 'mind' in Greek, is the faculty of intellectual apprehension and of intuitive thought. It is distinguished from discursive thought and applies to the apprehension of eternal intelligible substances and the first principles.[148]

Consequently, primordially, *nous*, meaning 'intellect or intelligence,' is a concept from classical Greek philosophy for the faculty of the human mind necessary for understanding what is true or real. *Nous* is therefore, a term used to describe the highest faculty of the human mind, associated with rational thought, understanding, and insight. In the Aristotelian understanding *nous* is the basic understanding or awareness that allows human beings to think rationally. For him, this was distinct from the processing of sensory perception, including the use of imagination and memory, which other animals can do, or perhaps which automated machines can also do.[149] The philosopher concludes that the *nous* is connected to a discussion of how the human mind sets definitions in a consistent and communicable way, and whether people must be born with some innate potential to understand the same universal categories in the same logical ways.

Now, let's re-visit our original question, how intelligent is AI? If the meaning of intelligence primordially is attributed to rational beings – as Aristotle asserts – can we still attribute the same to the automated machines like computers, which is actually an outcome of our human

---

[148] Britannica, T. Editors of Encyclopedia. "Nous," *Encyclopedia Britannica*, June 16, 2013. https://www.britannica.com/topic/nous.

[149] Aristotle, *De Anima (on the Soul)* Book III, Chapters 4-5.

rationality? For a number of decades, people have been talking about the extraordinary potential of Artificial Intelligence. **But is AI as intelligent as people say it is?** The idea that automated machines can think and learn like humans has captivated people from all walks of life. And with the recent advances in machine learning, AI is finally a talk of the day, especially in our emerging generations. And as we have asserted above, even the so-called Strong AI, which is claimed to operate like rational agents does not yet exist and remains a theoretical goal, or rather a wishing thinking!

It therefore, logically sound to argue that automated machines cannot think, reason, and remember as humans do. Instead, AI systems are programmed with specific goals in mind and can only act within the scope of those goals, with minimum novelty. John Searle's for instance, challenges the notion that a computer running a program can have a mind, consciousness, or understanding, regardless of its apparent ability to understand a certain language.[150] Epistemologically, several scholars have criticized the information generated through AI. For instance, Floridi argues that AI systems, relying on biased datasets, may produce results that reflect and perpetuate societal biases, raising questions about the reliability of their knowledge generation.[151] Other critics contend that the opacity of AI decision-making processes challenges traditional notions of epistemic authority and accountability, as it becomes difficult to interpret how conclusions are reached. Similarly, AI's ability to process vast amounts of data may lead to a superficial understanding that lacks deeper contextual or conceptual knowledge, questioning the depth of AI-driven insights.[152]

Therefore, whereas artificial intelligence (AI) exhibits intelligence in specific domains, it differs significantly from human intelligence in several fundamental ways. AI is often categorized as narrow intelligence, proficient in specific tasks but lacking the general cognitive abilities of humans. For instance, AI excels in tasks like image

---

[150] John R. Searle, Minds, Brains, and Programs, *Behavioral and Brain Sciences*, 3(3), 1980, 417-457

[151] Luciano Floridi, *The Logic of Information: A Theory of Philosophy as Conceptual Design* (Oxford: Oxford University Press, 2019), 215.

[152] Frank Pasquale, *The Black Box Society: The Secret Algorithms That Control Money and Information* (Cambridge, MA: Harvard University Press, 2015), 102.

recognition and language processing through algorithms and data analysis, but human intelligence encompasses a broad spectrum of abilities including learning, adaptation, creativity, emotional understanding, and ethical reasoning, which current AI systems cannot fully replicate.[153] While AI can process vast amounts of data and make predictions, it lacks the contextual understanding, common sense reasoning, and adaptability inherent in human cognition. Furthermore, human intelligence integrates sensory inputs, social interactions, and complex cognitive processes, contributing to creativity and emotional intelligence, aspects that current AI systems do not possess.[154] Conclusively, while AI presents a significant advancement in computational capabilities, it remains distinct from the multifaceted and adaptive intelligence exhibited by human beings.

The Pivotal Concerns of Philosophy of AI?

The philosophy of artificial intelligence attempts to answer questions such as; can a machine act intelligently? Can it solve problems that a person would solve by thinking? Can we consider human intelligence and machine intelligence to be the same? Can machines have minds, mental states and consciousness in the same sense that human beings have? Do machines have emotions, do they have feelings as humans do? Questions of this nature attract the divergent of AI researchers, cognitive scientists as well as philosophers. This part will attempt to explore some of the basic questions that philosophy of AI investigates.

The Nature of Intelligence of AI

One of the key area that philosophy of AI investigates is nature of intelligence that AI machines exhibits. Philosophers and scientists debate on what constitutes intelligence and whether AI can genuinely replicate or exceed human intelligence. Some argue that intelligence involves specific cognitive abilities, such as learning, reasoning, and

---

[153] Luciano Floridi, *The Logic of Information*, 215.

[154] Pasquale, Frank. *The Black Box Society: The Secret Algorithms That Control Money and Information*, (Cambridge, MA: Harvard University Press, 2015), 102.

problem-solving, and such abilities are attributed to rational agents. Still others consider intelligence to be a broader concept that includes emotional and social skills which are exhibited by human beings.[155]

Consciousness and Mind

On the question of consciousness and mind, a dominant issue in the philosophy of AI is whether machines can possess consciousness or a mind. Here, theories range from strong AI, which posits that machines could potentially achieve consciousness like that of human beings[156], to weak AI, which views machines as merely simulating human-like behaviour without true consciousness,[157] thus lacking possibility of machines 'being conscious' in the strict sense of the term. In a nutshell, the philosophy of AI questions whether AI systems can possess consciousness and subjective experiences like humans have. According to some scholar's consciousness is associated with biological processes, and thus AI machines lack such processes. For instance, a renowned philosopher of the mind, David Chalmers, explores the concept of consciousness and the 'hard problem' of explaining subjective experience, raising questions about whether AI can achieve true consciousness.[158]

Ethical and Moral Considerations

As AI systems become more autonomous, questions arise about who is morally responsible for their actions and decisions. Can machines be responsible moral agents? In his book, *Superintelligence: Paths, Dangers, Strategies,* Bostrom discusses the ethical implications of creating super intelligent machines, including the risks and challenges associated with developing AI that surpasses human intelligence.[159] As a whole, philosophy of AI questions the ethical and moral considerations of AI automated machines. To what extent should

---

[155] Marcus Hutter, *Universal Artificial Intelligence:* Sequential Decisions Based on Algorithmic Probability Springer: 2005, 18-24.

[156] Stuart Russell and Peter Norvig, *Artificial Intelligence: Modern Approach,* 935-937.

[157] Ibid.

[158] David J. Chelmers, *The Conscious Mind in Search of a Fundamental Theory,* (Oxford: Oxford University Press, 1996) 236.

[159] Nick Bostrom, *Superintelligence: Paths, Dangers, Strategies,* (Oxford: Oxford University Press, 2015), 45.

AI systems be allowed to make decisions without human intervention? This brings us to the whole issue of accountability and the potential risks of relinquishing too much control to AI.

Epistemology and Knowledge

Epistemology is the branch of philosophy concerned with the theory of knowledge. Strictly speaking, epistemology deals with questions regarding the nature, origin, scope, and limits of human knowledge. This being the case, the philosophy of AI poses epistemological concerns with regard to the nature and limits of knowledge as it pertains to AI. This includes understanding how AI systems acquire, process, and utilize information, and whether they can develop genuine understanding or wisdom.[160] Philosophers explore what it means to understand and whether AI systems merely mimic intelligence or if they truly comprehend the information. John McCarthy has written extensively on the epistemological problems of artificial intelligence. In his exploration, McCarthy questions whether epistemological facts can be represented in the memory of a computer, and what rules permit legitimate conclusions to be drawn from these facts.[161]

Potential Existential Risks

Philosophers have constantly been concerned about some potential risks associated with the development of super-intelligent AI. Super-intelligent AI refers to a hypothetical form of artificial intelligence that surpasses human intelligence across all fields, including creativity, problem-solving, and social intelligence. This concept involves AI systems that not only perform tasks better than the best human experts but also improve their capabilities autonomously,

---

[160] Bostrom, N., & Yudkowsky, E. *The Ethics of Artificial Intelligence*: In the *Cambridge Handbook of Artificial Intelligence* (Cambridge: University Press, 2014), 316-334.

[161] John McCarthy, "Epistemological Problems of Artificial Intelligence," Editor(s): Bonnie Lynn Webber, Nils J. Nilsson, *Readings in Artificial Intelligence,* (Morgan Kaufmann, 1981), 459-465. https://doi.org/10.1016/B978-0-934613-03-3.50035-0.

potentially leading to rapid and unprecedented advancements in technology and society.[162]

One argument expounded to explicate the risks of super-intelligent AI goes like this: "Human beings dominate other species because of the distinctive capabilities of human brain that other animals lack. If AI then, were to surpass humanity in general intelligence and become super-intelligent, then it could become difficult or impossible to control."[163] Just like we see the fate of gorillas depend on human goodwill, so this might also be the fate of humanity depending on the actions of machine's superintelligence. Bostrom discusses extensively on existential risks associated with advanced AI, emphasizing the importance of ethical considerations in the development of powerful artificial intelligences.[164]

Questions Related to Aesthetics and Creativity

Since the beginning of the 21st century, AI technologies have gradually entered the artistic realm. We witness the development of AI systems that aim to assess, evaluate and appreciate artifacts according to artistic and aesthetic criteria. The use of AI in creative fields raises questions the nature of artistic expression, creativity and the role of intuition and inspiration, which have traditionally been associated with human cognition.[165] We face the old question concerning the nature of creativity: what kind of recombination of ideas, unusual analogies, and conceptual connections which are considered the hallmark of originality? Can AI produce artworks? Could machines reach a point at which we consider them genuinely creative? We also need to investigate the challenges posed by AI-art to the notion of 'authorship,' who is the author of an artificially generated artifact?

---

[162] Nick Bostrom, *Superintelligence: Paths, Dangers, Strategies*, 45.

[163] Bostrom, *Superintelligence: Paths, Dangers*, 57.

[164] See Bostrom, *Superintelligence: Paths, Dangers*

[165] Emanuele Arielli & Lev Manovich, AI-Aesthetics and the Anthropocentric Myth of Creativity. NODES 1 (19-20). (2022).

Philosophy of Technology

The phrase 'philosophy of technology' was first used in the late 19th century by German-born philosopher and geographer Ernst Kapp, who published a book titled *Elements of a Philosophy of Technology*.[166] The philosophy of technology is a sub-branch of philosophy that studies the nature of technology and its social impacts. The philosophy of AI therefore, investigates the broader implications of technology on human life and values. Some 20th century philosophers have addressed the effects of modern technology on humanity. They view technology as central to modern life. Martin Heidegger, for instance, explored the 'hidden' nature of technology's essence in which he argues that <u>Gestell</u> or *Enframing*, which posed for humans what he called its greatest danger and thus its greatest possibility. Heiddeger's Essay on 'The Question Concerning Technology, 1954, has highly influenced the philosophy of technology.[167] Martin Heidegger, like a prophet of doom, foresaw the great dangers potentially inherent in the modern technological novelties, despite the great open possibilities that can evidently be seen. He thus warned that human thinking and existence should not be overtaken by machine thinking. Overall, Heidegger's analysis of technology emphasizes the need for critical reflection on how technological thinking influences human life and calls for a more profound engagement with the essence of technology to safeguard human freedom and authenticity.

An Exploration of Kantian Notion of Freewill

Kant's philosophy lays great emphasis on human autonomy and the moral responsibility that arises from the exercise of free will. Kant explores the question of freewill in the third section (Transition from Metaphysics of Morals to the Critique of Pure Practical Reason) of his seminal work, *Foundation on Metaphysics of Morals*. He opens the third section by making one of the two connections that his argument

---

[166] Erwin Marquit, "Technology, Philosophy of" Encyclopedia of Physics, Vol. 13, (1995), 417-29

[167] Martin Heidegger, "The Question Concerning Technology and other Essays" (1977) 3-35.

requires. In his argument, he posits that the will is the causality of a rational beings, for our will determines our actions, and it is through our actions that we have effects in the world. If the actions of the will, that is, its choices and decisions, were in turn determined by the laws of nature, then it would not be a free will.[168] For instance, suppose that all our choices were determined by a psychological law of nature, say, 'a person's will is always determined by the strength of his desires. Although one would always do what they most strongly desire, their will would not, according to Kant's definition, be free. According to Kant, a free person is one whose actions are not determined by any external force, not even by his own desires. For, having a will he says, is the same thing as being rational, and having a free will means having a will that is not influenced by external forces.[169]

The above explanation is merely a negative conception of freedom. But Kant continues to point to us a more positive conception of freedom in his second argument. He asserts that the will is a cause, and the concept of causality includes the idea of acting according to laws – since we identify something as a cause by observing the regularity of its effects, the idea of a cause which functions randomly is a contradiction. To put it another way, the will is practical reason, and we cannot conceive a practical reason that chooses and acts for no reason. Since reasons are derived from principles, then, the will must have a principle. A free will must therefore have its own law or principle, which it gives to itself. Thus, it must be an autonomous will. An autonomous will according to Kant, is one that operates based on reason and rational principles rather than being driven by external forces or internal inclinations. It reflects the idea that moral agents should act out of respect for moral law, which is derived from rationality.[170]

In summary, because a freewill is not merely pushed around by external forces, external forces do not provide laws for a free will. We can, therefore, deduce that the only source of law for a freewill is that will itself. This is Kant's notion of autonomy. Kant defines autonomy

---

[168] Immanuel Kant, *Groundwork of the Metaphysics of Morals*, Tras. &Ed. by Mary Gregor. Cambridge: Cambridge University Press, 1997, 25.

[169] Immanuel Kant, *Groundwork of the Metaphysics of Morals*, 26.

[170] Immanuel Kant, *Groundwork of the Metaphysics of Morals*, 6.

as the capacity to legislate moral laws for oneself through reason. In the *Groundwork for the Metaphysics of Morals*, he writes, "Autonomy of the will is the only thing that can be considered a good without qualification... For the will is a law-giving member of the kingdom of ends."[171] Thus, Kant's notion of freedom of the will requires that we are morally self-legislating; that we impose the moral law on ourselves. Finally, Kant thinks that this positive understanding of freedom amounts to the same thing as the categorical imperative (CI). Categorical Imperative requires individuals to act according to principles that they themselves could rationally will to be universal laws. Thus, in the same work he states, he states, "Act only according to that maxim whereby you can, at the same time, will that it should become a universal law."[172] Following Kant's explication here, we can thus conclude that a free will and a will under moral law, which is regulated by CI, are one and the same.

Examining AI Vis-à-Vis Kant's Notion of Free will

Examining the Philosophy of AI through the lens of Immanuel Kant's notion of free will involve exploring some key areas of Kantian Philosophy, especially in the area of autonomy, rationality and moral agents. Needlessly to say, Kant's conception of free will is deeply intertwined with his notions of autonomy, rationality, and moral agency. This article has already asserted that the Kantian moral philosophy puts great emphasis on human autonomy and moral responsibility that flows from the exercise of freewill. Applying these notions to AI may raise important questions about the nature of AI, its autonomy and ethical implications of its actions. Kant's Moral philosophy, particularly in the *Groundwork of the Metaphysics of Morals* and the *Critique of Pure Reason*, provides a framework for understanding how moral agents, including AI, might be evaluated in terms of these concepts.

Kant argues that humans possess a unique form of autonomy which is grounded in rationality and the ability to act according to self-

---

[171] Immanuel Kant, *Groundwork of the Metaphysics of Morals*, 7.
[172] Immanuel Kant, *Groundwork of the Metaphysics of Morals*, 30.

imposed moral principles. Autonomy for Kant, implies acting in accordance with the moral law that one gives themselves. According to him, autonomy is the ability to act according to one's rational will, which is distinct from mere natural causation or external influences. In the *Groundwork of the Metaphysics of Morals*, Kant argues: "Autonomy of the will is the only one that can be a priori, and it is the ground of all moral laws."[173] This implies that a being is morally responsible if it acts out of a sense of duty governed by rational laws it has given to itself.

The second question in this discussion is on the moral agent and rationality of the action. Kant's notion of moral agency is closely linked with the capacity for rational self-governance. He states that a moral agent must be capable of acting according to the moral law, which is based on reason rather than empirical desires. According to him, moral agent involves the ability to act in accordance with moral principles and take responsibility for one's actions. A morally good action in Kant's view is defined by its adherence to the moral law, which is grounded in reason and autonomy. In the *Critique of Pure Reason*, Kant categorically states that, "the moral law within us is not derived from the natural world but from the rational will."[174] Therefore, moral actions are those performed out of a sense of duty and in accordance with the categorical imperative – acting according to the maxim that one would wish all other rational agents to follow, as if it were a universal law.

Critiquing AI in the Light of Kantian's Notion of Freewill

A close examination of Kant's notions to AI presents obvious unique perennial challenges. While AI systems can exhibit complex behaviour and decision-making processes, they lack autonomy in the Kantian sense because they do not legislate moral laws for themselves. Instead, they follow programmed instructions and algorithms designed by humans. In his article, "Autonomy and the Role of AI in Decision,"

---

[173] Immanuel Kant, *Groundwork of the Metaphysics of Morals*, 32.
[174] Kant, Immanuel. *Critique of Pure Reason*. Translated by Norman Kemp Smith, St. Martin's Press, 1965, A 813/B 841.

Binns, argues that AI systems, despite their advanced capabilities, lack true autonomy. They operate within the constraints defined by their algorithms and data inputs and do not possess self-awareness or subjective experiences that inform autonomous decision-making in humans.[175] Conclusively, AI systems do not possess autonomy as Kant describes it. They do not create or follow moral laws out of rational deliberation but operate based on pre-defined rules and data-driven algorithms. Thus, they lack the capacity for self-legislation and moral reasoning.

On the question of rationality and moral agency, we also have inevitable divergence views. According to Kantian ethics, rationality involves the ability to act according to universal moral principles. Since AI lacks true rationality and moral understanding, perhaps, it may not be considered a moral agent in the Kantian sense. Instead, AI can be seen as a tool used by rational agents (humans) who are responsible for making ethical decisions and using AI in a morally permissible way. While **rationality** involves the ability to reason logically and make decisions based on coherent principles, AI is interpreted through the lens of how algorithms process information and make decisions. Scholars has criticized AI systems which follow pre-programmed algorithms that aim to maximize certain objectives based on data. However, they argue that these algorithms are not infallible and can exhibit biases if the training data is skewed or incomplete.[176] In contrary, human rationality is influenced by emotions, experiences, and complex social contexts, which are not currently replicable by AI. AI's rationality is confined to the scope of its programming and data processing abilities.[177]

---

[175] Richard Binns, "Autonomy and the Role of AI in Decision-Making." *Journal of AI Research*, (2021). 68, 112-125.

[176] Kroll, S., et al. (2016). "Accountable Algorithms." *University of Pennsylvania Law Review*, 165(3), pp. 633-705.

[177] Hubert L. Dreyfus, *What Computers Still Can't Do: A Critique of Artificial Reason?* MIT Press, 2016), 98-120.

Some Ethical Considerations

Kant ethics places a strong emphasis on treating individuals as ends in themselves and not merely as a means to an end. Kantian ethics asserts that individuals have intrinsic worth and should be treated with respect, meaning they should never be used merely as tools to achieve another goal. Thus, for him, respect for the dignity of rational beings is a central theme. Unfortunately, according to Binns, AI systems are often designed to optimize processes, enhance efficiencies, or extract data, which can sometimes lead to the exploitation of individuals for the sake of broader goals.[178] Kant's stance is that using AI systems to exploit personal data without regard for individual privacy or to manipulate behavior could be seen as treating people merely as means to an end.

AI systems used for surveillance or data collection can infringe on personal privacy, potentially treating individuals as mere sources of data rather than respecting their autonomy and dignity. Besides, AI systems can perpetuate or exacerbate biases, leading to unjust treatment of individuals based on race, gender, or other attributes. This could be viewed as treating individuals unfairly, rather than respecting their inherent worth.[179] In general, ethical concerns today arise when AI is used in ways that potentially undermine human dignity or even treat individuals solely as a means to achieve certain desired ends. For instance, decisions made by AI systems that impact individuals' lives may lack the depth of ethical consideration that Kantian ethics demands.

Conclusion

Conclusively, an evaluation of the philosophy of Artificial Intelligence (AI) through the lens of Kantian free will has raised several key pertinent issues. In the first place, Kant's philosophy emphasizes the centrality of autonomy and rationality that defines the clear notion

---

[178] Binns, R. "Fairness in Machine Learning." *Proceedings of the 2018 CHI Conference on Human Factors in Computing Systems*, 2018.

[179] Virginia Dignum, Ethics in artificial intelligence: Introduction to the special issue. *AI & Society, 33*(3), 2018, 321-326. https://doi.org/10.1007/s00146-018-0802-4

of free will. These two concepts are deeply tied to moral responsibility and the capacity for ethical decision-making. AI, as we know it today, operates within the bounds of pre-programmed processes that lacks the intrinsic autonomy and rationality that are attributable to human agents. Needlessly to say, it is true that AI systems can simulate decision-making processes, but their actions are ultimately determined by human-designed parameters that have no capacity for self-legislation or moral reasoning.

Therefore, despite its growing complexity and potential, AI cannot possess true free will in the Kantian sense. It only operates within deterministic frameworks, where its 'choices' are the product of external manipulation instead of internal rational deliberation. Overall, the conclusion of this article suggests that while AI can be a powerful tool for increasing human competences, it remains fundamentally distinct from humans because it lacks a free will. This calls for a need to observe ethical boundaries as we celebrate the current AI technologies. Kantian notion of freewill therefore, provides a dependable lens through which we can assess the potentials and limits of AI technologies in the light of the human freewill.

References:

ARIELLI, Emanuele & MANOVICH Lev, "AI-Aesthetics and the Anthropocentric Myth of Creativity. NODES 1" (19-20). (2022).

ARISTOTLE, *De Anima (on the Soul)* Book III.

BRITANNICA, T. Editors of Encyclopedia. "Nous," *Encyclopedia Britannica*, June 16, 2013. https://www.britannica.com/topic/nous

BROWN Clair & LINDEN Greg. "Two Decades of Recommender Systems at Amazon.com." *IEEE Internet Computing*, 21(3), (2017). 12-18.

BOSTROM, Nick. *Superintelligence: Paths, Dangers, Strategie*. Oxford: Oxford University Press, 2015.

BOSTROM, N., & YUDKOWSKY, E. *The Ethics of Artificial Intelligence: In the Cambridge Handbook of Artificial Intelligence*. Cambridge: University Press, 2014. 316-334

COPELAND, Jack. (Ed.) *The Essential Turing: The Ideas that gave Birth to the Computer Age*. Oxford: Clarendon Press, 2004.

CHATTERJEE et al., "Evolution of Artificial Intelligence and Its Impact on Human Rights: From Sociolegal Perspective," International Journal of Law and Management, 62(2): January, 2021, 184-205.

COPELAND, Jack. (Ed.) *The Essential Turing: The Ideas that gave Birth to the Computer Age*. Oxford: Clarendon Press, 2004.

CHATTERJEE et al., "Evolution of Artificial Intelligence and Its Impact on Human Rights: From Sociolegal Perspective," *International Journal of Law and Management*, 62(2): January, 2021, 184-205.

CHELMERS, J. David. *The Conscious Mind in Search of a Fundamental Theory*. Oxford: Oxford University Press, 1996.

_____, *The Conscious Mind in Search of a Fundamental Theory*. Oxford: Oxford University Press, 1996.

DREYFUS, Hubert L. *What Computers Still Can't Do: A Critique of Artificial Reason?* MIT Press, 2016.

DIGNUM, Virginia. Ethics in artificial intelligence: Introduction to the special issue. *AI & Society*, 33(3), 2018, 321-326. https://link.springer.com/article/10.1007/s10676-018-9450-z

FLORIDI, Luciano. *The Logic of Information: A Theory of Philosophy as Conceptual Design*. Oxford: Oxford University Press, 2019.

HEIDEGGER, Martin. "The Question Concerning Technology and other Essays" (1977) 3-35.

KANT, Immanuel. *Groundwork of the Metaphysics of Morals, Tras. &Ed.* by Mary Gregor. Cambridge: Cambridge University Press, 1997, 25.

____, *Critique of Pure Reason.* Translated by Norman Kemp Smith, St. Martin's Press, 1965.

KROLL, S., et al. (2016). "Accountable Algorithms." *University of Pennsylvania Law Review*, 165(3), pp. 633-705.

LINDEN, J. Stanton. *The Alchemy Reader: From Hermes Trismegistus to Isaac Newton.* New York: Cambridge University, 2003

LITMAN, Todd. *Autonomous Vehicle Implementation Predictions Implications for Transport Planning*, (Victoria Transport Policy Institute, 2020.

MAYOR, Adrienne. *God's and Robots: Myths, Machines and Ancient Dreams of Technology.* New York: Princeton University Press, 2018.

MARQUIT, Erwin. "Technology, Philosophy of" Encyclopedia of Physics, Vol. 13, (1995), 417-29

MCCARTHY, John. "Epistemological Problems of Artificial Intelligence," Editor(s): Bonnie Lynn Webber, Nils J. Nilsson, *Readings in Artificial Intelligence.* Morgan Kaufmann, 1981, 459-465. https://doi.org/10.1016/B978-0-934613-03-3.50035-0

NILS, Nilsson. *The Quest for Artificial Intelligence.* Cambridge University Press, 2010.

PASQUALE, Frank. *The Black Box Society: The Secret Algorithms That Control Money and Information.* Cambridge, MA: Harvard University Press, 2015.

RHODIOUS, Apollonious. *The Argonautika: Expanded Edition.* California: University of California

PRESS, 2007. Searle, J. R. (1980). Minds, brains, and programs. *Behavioral and Brain Sciences, 3*(3), 417-457

STUART Russell, J., and NORVIG Peter. *Artificial Intelligence: A Modern Approach.* 3rd ed., Prentice Hall, 2010.

Human-Artificial Intelligence Relationship a Moral Inquiry from a Heideggerian Perspective

Barasa Nasambu Joy, LSOSF, holds a Master's degree in Philosophy, and is, currently a PhD student at The Catholic University of Eastern Africa (CUEA), in Nairobi-Kenya.

Abstract

This paper examines the evolving relationship between Humans and Artificial Intelligence (AI) through the philosophical lens of Martin Heidegger. It involves delving into Heidegger's existential phenomenology which emphasizes the human experience of being-in-the-world of technology. Examining the moral implications of the growing integration of AI into various aspects of human society, this inquiry seeks to unravel the existential questions surrounding the ethical dimensions of human-AI interactions. The investigation begins by expounding Heidegger's concept of "enframing" or "Gestel," (German), and how it applies to AI technology that shapes and controls the way we perceive and interact with the world. It then probes into the ethical considerations arising from the deployment of AI in fields of social communication, healthcare, finance, and education among others. The exploration encompasses the questions of consciousness and moral agency, responsibility, and the potential transformation of human identity in the face of advancing AI. Additionally, the paper investigates the notion of "human authenticity" from the Heideggerian perspective, examining how individuals remain true to themselves while confronting their existence in the face of emerging technology, and dealing with germane questions about the role of AI in shaping our well-being. Therefore, this inquiry intends to contribute to the ongoing debate on the ethical implications of AI, thus advocating for a thoughtful and reflective approach to the development and implementation of AI technologies, grounded on an awareness of their profound impact on the moral fabric of human existence. This inquiry is purely qualitative.

Key Words: Artificial Intelligence, Enframing, Authenticity, Consciousness, Responsibility.

Introduction

The integration of Artificial Intelligence (AI) into various aspects of human life has raised profound philosophical and ethical questions. This has necessitated a critical examination of the evolving relationship between humans and AI through the lens of Martin Heidegger's existential phenomenology. By exploring Heidegger's concept of "enframing" (German: *Gestel*), this inquiry aims to unravel the existential and ethical dimensions of human-AI interactions. The examination extends to the moral implications of AI deployment in social communication, healthcare, finance, and education among other domains. Moreover, the paper delves into the questions of consciousness, moral agency, responsibility, and the potential transformation of human identity in the context of advancing AI. Lastly, it explores the Heideggerian notion of "human authenticity," emphasizing how individuals can remain true to themselves while navigating the challenges posed by emerging technologies.

What is Artificial Intelligence?

Artificial Intelligence (AI), sometimes called machine intelligence, is different from natural intelligence displayed by humans. Driven by the desire to enhance efficiency, solve complex problems, and innovate in various fields, man has invented AI after acknowledging the limitations of his intelligence that is affected by issues like emotions and amnesia among others. However, this does not mean that AI surpasses human intelligence, since all AI advancements are fostered by human intelligence for scientific and technological growth.

Stuart Russel and Peter Norvig define AI as the study of agents that receive information from their environment and take action to achieve their goals. The term "agent" in this context refers to anything that can be considered perceiving its environment through sensors and acting upon that environment through actuators.[180] Agents of AI may include smart home technological devices like computers and phones, robots, automated machines, search engines like google and chatbots, and medical diagnostic systems among others. Though AI is a subset of technology that require human intelligence, the word technology will be used interchangeably with AI in this paper, in reference to agents of AI.

It's worth noting that AI attempts to model and apply the intelligence of the human mind for problem solving, learning, and research, among others. AI systems can complement human capabilities, fostering collaboration between humans and machines with the aim of leveraging the strengths of both to achieve more than what could accomplish. However, ethical issues may arise when one overreaches the other. Heidegger's existential phenomenology can help us to carry out a moral inquiry in the issue of Human-AI relationship.

Heidegger's Existential Phenomenology: Unframing and Dasein's Being-in-the-World

Heidegger is renowned for his existential phenomenology, a philosophical approach that explores the nature of human existence and the way individuals experience the world they live in, that is, *Dasein's Being-in-the-world*. As outlined in his seminal work *Being and Time*, Heidegger's existential phenomenology seeks to understand the fundamental structures of human existence and ways in which individuals engage with their surroundings, referred to as the environmentality and worldhood.[181] Existential phenomenology, therefore, involves an examination of the individual's subjective experience, emphasizing the concept of *Dasein*, which is translated as "existence" or "being there." Heidegger argues that being-in-the-world

---

[180] Stuart Russel and Peter Norvig, *Artificial Intelligence: A Modern Approach*, 3rd Ed., (Boston, London: Prentice Hall, 2010), 34.

[181] Martin Heidegger, *Being and Time*, Trans., John Macquarrie & Edward Robinson (New York and London: Harper & Row Publishers, 1962), 91ff. Henceforth referred to as Heidegger, *Being and Time*.

is a way in which *Dasein's* character is defined existentially.[182] In this context, understanding human existence requires an analysis of the individual's unique, lived experiences, rather than abstract or theoretical considerations.

Heidegger's existential phenomenology therefore provides a valuable framework for understanding the human experience in the age of technology, specifically AI. Central to his phenomenology, is the concept of "enframing" (*Gestel*) discussed in his essay: *The Question Concerning Technology*. We need to understand what Heidegger meant by technology and enframing.

Technology, according to Heidegger, is not merely a collection of tools or machines; rather, it is a mode of revealing or uncovering the world. He uses the German word *Technik* to refer to technology, and his exploration goes beyond the common understanding of technology as a means to an end. Instead, Heidegger seeks to cognize technology's essence and its impact on human existence, that is, how technology reveals and shapes our understanding of the world.[183] In the process of cognition, he arrives at the concept of "enframing" as the essence of technology after reflecting on other concepts like challenging forth and revealing, standing-reserve and instrumentality, traditional craft, and modern technology.[184]

Heidegger held that, in the course of uncovering the world, technology challenges forth and brings to light particular aspects of the world, shaping our understanding of reality. However, this revealing is not neutral, it occurs within a specific context and mode. Furthermore, the same technology is viewed as a standing-reserve, where, in the essence of technology, the world is seen as a resource waiting to be ordered, controlled, and utilized for human purposes. This perspective reduces things to their utility and instrumental value. Heidegger therefore contrasts traditional craftsmanship with modern technology, where in traditional craftsmanship, the artisan engages with materials in a more personal and responsive manner, whereas in modern

---

[182] Heidegger, *Being and Time*, 92.

[183] Martin Heidegger, *The Question Concerning Technology and Other Essays*, Trans., William Lovitt (New York and London: Garland Publishing, INC., 1977), 3-14.

[184] Heidegger, *The Question Concerning Technology and Other Essays*, 15-20

technology, there is a more calculative and efficient approach that reduces things to standing-reserve for exploitation. This, he says, is influenced by enframing; that which reduces things to their utility and manipulability, stripping them of their own inherent essence or meaning

Enframing is presented as the essence of technology, the overarching mode in which technology operates, revealing the world as a standing-reserve. It is not just a particular technological device or system, but a way of understanding and relating to the world, a mode of revealing that characterizes the essence of modern technology. The concept of enframing is therefore used by Heidegger to critique modern technology and its potential dehumanizing effects. He contends that enframing is a supreme danger, that which reduces everything, including human existence, to a mere resource for technological efficiency.[185] By emphasizing the way technology reveals the world as a standing-reserve, he provokes us to reflect on the broader implications of the technological mode of being and its impact on human identity and existence.

In the context of AI, enframing emphasizes the aspect of instrumentalization of the world, viewing it as an object to be exploited for efficiency and productivity. In analysing human-AI interactions, enframing becomes crucial in unraveling both existential and ethical dimensions. While enframing alters existential experience by reducing human existence to a calculative and instrumental relationship with the world from the existential dimension, it poses ethical challenges as it can lead to a dehumanizing relationship, prioritizing efficiency and utility over human values. In this case, human existence is reduced to a resource within the enframed perspective, thus, may lead to ethical dilemmas in AI design and usage where decisions are driven more by technical efficiency than by considerations of human well-being, dignity, and moral values. As technology, especially AI, becomes more integrated into everyday life, there is a risk of individuals becoming alienated from a genuine, authentic experience of being, since their interactions are increasingly mediated and shaped by technological processes. In this sense, carrying out a moral inquiry into the

---

[185] Heidegger, *The Question Concerning Technology and Other Essays*, 26.

deployment of AI is inevitable to ensure technology serves humanity in a required manner.

Ethical Considerations in Human-AI Interactions

The integration of AI in various sectors necessitates a careful examination of the moral implications involved. The investigation into the moral dimensions of AI deployment in social communication, healthcare, education, among others, scrutinizes the questions of consciousness and moral agency, exploring whether AI possesses a form of autonomy that warrants ethical consideration. Delving into the responsibility associated with AI development and usage, emphasizes the need for a reflective approach to mitigate potential ethical pitfalls.

Ethical Issues Associated with AI Deployment in Social Media and Communication

AI is deployed in numerous areas of social media and communication platforms to enhance user experiences, streamline processes, and optimize content delivery. This includes: content recommendation in algorithmic feeds and content suggestions where social media platforms use AI algorithms to curate personalized content feeds based on user preferences, engagement history, and behavior, and help in suggesting relevant content and other information to improve overall user experience.[186] It is also used in chatbots and virtual assistants (computerized programmes) where businesses use AI-powered chatbots to provide automatic responses to customers, suggesting replies and providing information on messaging applications. AI is deployed for content moderation, that is, detecting and filtering inappropriate or offensive content to ensure safer online. Other sections where AI is deployed are voice and image recognition, image and video analysis, data analysis and insight provision, automated advertisements, and provision of network security such as fraud detection among others. The deployment of AI in this area is facilitated by machine learning algorithms, natural language

---

[186] Russel and Norvig, *Artificial Intelligence: A Modern Approach*, 872.

processing, computer vision, and other AI techniques that enable systems to learn and adapt user-based interactions and data patterns.[187]

AI deployment in the above areas is intended to assist social media users. However, it brings out numerous ethical issues that can impact individuals and society. These include:

I. Privacy and Data Protection: personal data can be used for advertisements, thus, ethical considerations obtaining informed consent from data owners and protecting user privacy.[188]

II. Algorithmic Biases and discrimination: while AI algorithms inherit biases from training data, ethical concerns involve ensuring fair treatment of all users.[189]

III. Content Moderation and Censorship: AI content moderation can be subjective, and so there is need for transparency in moderation policies avoiding undue censorship.

IV. Misinformation: AI can involve in the malpractice of spreading fake news and misinforming the users. In this case, social media platforms should take responsibility of addressing misinformation that impact the public domain.

V. User Manipulation: AI algorithms always seek to optimize user engagement leading to concerns about manipulation and addictive user experiences. In this sense, users may have limited understanding and control over how AI algorithms shape their online experiences. Ethical considerations involve balancing user engagement with the potential for unintended behavioral consequences, and providing users with transparency, control mechanisms, and the ability to understand and influence algorithmic decisions. User autonomy and control is key.[190]

VI. Cybersecurity: sometimes AI may fail to detect adversarial attacks and user manipulation of its data. Ethical concerns involve ensuring the security of AI systems to prevent data

---

[187] Russel and Norvig, *Artificial Intelligence: A Modern Approach*, 860 ff.

[188] Bruce Schneir, *Data and Goliath: The Hidden Battles to Collect your Data and Control Your World*, (New York, London: W.W. Norton &Company, 2015), 68,92-93. Henceforth, Schneir, *Data and Goliath*

[189] Schneir, *Data and Goliath*, 94-95.

[190] Schneir, *Data and Goliath*,75-77, 83.

breaches and cyber threats.[191] Bruce Schneir suggests the use of encryption and cryptography in general to defend data from attack.[192]

VII. Social Disconnect: when users are preoccupied with social media, human-human interaction, and social values lose meaning. Schneir accounts: "This has changed. Companies have fewer face-to-face meetings. Friends socialize online. My wife and I have intimate conversations by text message. We all behave as if these conversations were ephemeral, but they're not."[193] There is a need to make proper use of AI for social good.[194]

The deployment of AI can have unintended consequences which need to be anticipated and addressed in time. Addressing the above ethical issues requires ongoing efforts from various platform developers, policymakers, and users to establish responsible guidelines for the deployment of AI in social media and communication. Balancing innovation with ethical considerations is essential for creating a digital environment that fosters trust, inclusivity, and positive societal impact.

Ethical Issues Associated with AI Deployment in Healthcare

In the current society, Machine Learning (ML), a subset of AI, has been the most popular approach of current AI healthcare applications since it allows computational systems to learn from data and improve their performance without being explicitly programmed.[195] This AI technique is used in areas such as imaging and diagnostics, drug discovery and development, patient monitoring, robot-assisted surgery, mental health and other diseases detection, and administrative

---

[191] Schneir, *Data and Goliath*, 99.

[192] Schneir, *Data and Goliath*, 104.

[193] Schneir, *Data and Goliath*, 93.

[194] Lucian Floridi, *The Ethics of Artificial Intelligence: Principles, Challenges, and Opportunities*, (Oxford: Oxford University Press, 2023), 142.

[195] Sara K Gerke, Timmo Minssen, and Glenn Cohen, "Ethical and legal challenges of artificial intelligence-driven healthcare," in *Artificial Intelligence in Healthcare*, (Elsevier 2020), P.295-336. DOI: https://doi.org/10.1016/B978-0-12-818438-7.00012-5

workflow automation. The same is used in designing artificial organs and monitoring how they function.

According to the analysis of Gerke, Minssen, and Cohen of the United States' and Europe's healthcare system where AI is deployed, there are various ethical challenges involved. The primary challenges include informed consent to use, safety and transparency, algorithmic fairness and biases, and data protection and privacy cybersecurity.[196] These ethical challenges apply universally and worldwide. To realize the tremendous potential of AI to transform healthcare for the better, they suggest that stakeholders in the AI field, including AI makers, clinicians, patients, ethicists, and legislators, must be engaged in the ethical and legal debate on how AI is successfully implemented in practice.[197] Therefore, agencies should consider ten principles when formulating approaches to AI applications. These are: public trust in AI, public participation, scientific integrity and information quality, risk assessment and management, benefits and costs, flexibility, fairness and non-discrimination, disclosure and transparency, safety and security, and interagency coordination[198]

Ethical Issues Associated with AI Deployment in Education

The education sector has adopted AI in teaching and learning processes, automated grading and assessment systems, predictive analysis of student performance, content creation, and administrative tasks, among others. In this context, AI systems are understood as the algorithmic models that carry out cognitive or perceptual functions in the world that were previously reserved for thinking, judging, and reasoning human beings.[199] AI is increasingly making an impact on

---

[196] Gerke, Minssen, and Cohen, "Ethical and legal challenges of artificial intelligence-driven healthcare," 295.

[197] Gerke, Minssen, and Cohen, "Ethical and legal challenges of artificial intelligence-driven healthcare," 295.

[198] Gerke, Minssen, and Cohen, "Ethical and legal challenges of artificial intelligence-driven healthcare," 297.

[199] Wayne Holmes et al, "Artificial Intelligence and Education: A critical view through the lens of human rights, democracy and the rule of law," *Council of Europe*, (November2022), 16. https://rm.coe.int/artificial-intelligence-and-education-a-critical-view-through-the-lens/1680a886bd

education, bringing opportunities as well as numerous threats. It has been noted that the 2019 Council of Europe's Committee of Ministers adopted a recommendation on digital citizenship education in which a key focus was the application of artificial intelligence (AI) in educational contexts.[200] The recommendation states:

> *AI, like any other tool, offers many opportunities but also carries with it many threats, which make it necessary to take human rights principles into account in the early design of its application. Educators must be aware of the strengths and weaknesses of AI in learning, so as to be empowered, not overpowered by technology in their digital citizenship education practices. AI, via machine learning and deep learning, can enrich education ... By the same token, developments in the AI field can deeply impact interactions between educators and learners and among citizens at large, which may undermine the very core of education, that is, the fostering of free will and independent and critical thinking via learning opportunities ... Although it seems premature to make wider use of AI in learning environments, professionals in education and school staff should be made aware of AI and the ethical challenges it poses in the context of schools.[201]*

Going through this report raises our concern to explore the human-AI relationship in education and its moral implications. The main challenge of using AI is in the ability of students to rely fully on AI for their learning and even exams. This comes with several implications.

I. Student Autonomy and Agency: excessive reliance on AI tools may diminish the role of educators where students do not need to attend lessons to acquire knowledge, and encourages malpractices in exams and in research, since students rely fully on AI for quick knowledge, limiting their critical thinking and problem-solving skills

---

[200] Wayne Holmes et al, "Artificial Intelligence and Education, ...," 11

[201] Council of Europe, Recommendation CM/Rec of the Committee of Ministers to member States on developing and promoting digital citizenship education, (2019)10 https://search.coe.int/cm/Pages/result_details.aspx?ObjectID=090000168098de08

II. Job Displacement: The introduction of AI in education may impact employability of educators and support staff, since their presence and efforts will be meaningless.

III. Unequal Access to AI Education: Students with limited access to AI education may face disadvantages in the future job market.

IV. Long-term Effects on Learning, especially narrowing of the curriculum: AI systems might focus on quantifiable metrics, potentially neglecting the broader aspects of education such as creativity, critical thinking, and social skills.

It has been noted that in contrast to health, where there are long-established ethical principles and codes of practice with regard to the treatment of human subjects, education (apart from university research) does not have the same universal approach or commonly accepted model of ethics. Much of the discussion on ethics of AI frames learners as data subjects, not as people. Accordingly, although a data protection impact assessment is required, commercial players and schools are able to engage children with AI-driven systems without any ethical or other risk assessment.[202]

According to Holmes, ethical inquiry in this area should focus on teacher expectations, of resource allocations (including teacher expertise), of behavior and discipline, of the accuracy and validity of assessments, of what constitutes useful knowledge, of teacher roles, of power relations between teachers and their students, and of particular approaches to pedagogy (teaching and learning, such as instructionism and constructivism).[203]

Addressing ethical challenges therefore requires a collaborative effort involving educators, policymakers, technologists, and other stakeholders to ensure that AI in education is deployed in a responsible and equitable manner. Regular ethical assessments, transparency in AI system design, and ongoing dialogue are essential components of a responsible approach to integrating AI into the education sector.

---

[202] Wayne Holmes et al, "Artificial Intelligence and Education, …," 42.
[203] Wayne Holmes et al, "Artificial Intelligence and Education, …," 42

Consciousness, Moral Agency, Responsibility, and Human Identity in the Face of AI

Although Heidegger did not specifically address artificial intelligence in his works, his philosophical insights provide a foundation for exploring the questions of consciousness, moral agency, responsibility, and the potential transformation of human identity in the context of advancing AI. Heidegger lived at a time when AI did not exist. However, his key ideas from the technological essays can be used to analyze the following issues in AI:

I. *Consciousness and Technology:* Heidegger's concept of "enframing" as discussed in his work, *The Question Concerning Technology*, referring to the way technology shapes our perception of the world, is relevant. He argues that man has failed to encounter himself and understand his essence in the face of technology. As technology becomes more integrated into human life, it contributes to a new way of understanding being and its consciousness; a state of awareness and responsiveness, in its way of being-in-the-world.[204] Heidegger therefore challenges the traditional view of technology as a neutral tool, suggesting that technology, including artificial intelligence, shapes our understanding of the world. By this he maintains that the root of impoverishment is the hegemony of the theoretical attitude, according to which reality consists in an "external world" of physical objects to be known or manipulated and which stands over against the "internal world" of human consciousness.[205] This means that the real vulnerability that we face emanates not from technology itself but from the technological understanding of being, which also constitutes its essence.

II. *Moral Agency and Responsibility:* Exploring the essence and definition of technology as a means to an end and a human activity, Heidegger says that our relationship with technology is a kind of instrumentalization. In this case, human beings have the power to experience technology within its bounds, for to posit

---

[204] Heidegger, *The Question Concerning Technology and Other Essays*, 27.

[205] Stephen Michelman, *Historical Dictionary of Existentialism*, (Lanham: The Scarecrow Press. Inc, 2008), 61.

ends, procure and utilize the means to them is a human activity. Therefore, Heidegger urges individuals to confront the challenges that technology poses to human existence. He asserts that "everywhere we remain unfree and chained to technology, whether we passionately affirm or deny it. But we are delivered over to it in the worst possible way when we regard it as something neutral."[206] This quote emphasizes the importance of acknowledging the impact of technology and taking responsibility for its consequences.

III. *Transformation of Human Identity:* As AI advances, the potential transformation of human identity becomes a pressing concern. Heidegger's philosophy underscores the idea that technology shapes our understanding of self and the world. The integration of AI into various aspects of human life may lead to a transformation of identity, as individuals interact with intelligent systems and incorporate them into their daily existence. This transformation could involve changes in perception, relationships, and even the way individuals define their purpose.

Human Identity in the Face of AI

Heidegger's concept of authenticity is central to his philosophy. The increasing integration of AI may pose challenges to human authenticity, as individuals interact with artificial entities that simulate human-like behaviors. The question emerges: can humans maintain an authentic existence in the face of AI, or does the presence of intelligent machines lead to a superficial understanding of authenticity? In his discourse, Heidegger held that conscience attests not only to the fact that I am affected by my own-most potentiality-for-Being, but it also testifies to the fact that I am dominated by it in my Being.[207] Therefore, "when the call of conscience is understood, lostness in the "they" is revealed. Resoluteness brings *Dasein* back to its own-most potentiality for Being-Its-Self. When one has an understanding of Being-towards-death, towards death as one's own-most possibility, one's potentiality-for-Being

---

[206] Heidegger, *The Question Concerning Technology and Other Essays*, 4.
[207] Heidegger, *Being and Time*, 312ff.

becomes authentic and wholly transparent."[208] The conscience is an important element in understanding how external influences, including AI, may affect human authenticity, hence prevent him from losing himself. Therefore, individuals can remain true to themselves while navigating the challenges posed by emerging technologies.

Ethical Framework for AI Development

Heidegger's philosophy prompts us to seek a deeper understanding of the essence of technology and explore ethical frameworks that can guide the development and deployment of AI. The responsibility for shaping technology in accordance with human values becomes crucial. This task would involve questioning the essence of AI, understanding its impact on human existence, and ensuring that it aligns with a vision of a more authentic and meaningful life. According to Heidegger, we must be ready to allow ourselves to be thwarted by technology at any time, but question its impact on human life, for questioning is the piety of thought.[209]

Conclusion

This work has examined the evolving relationship between Humans and Artificial Intelligence (AI) through the philosophical lens of Heidegger. It involved delving into his existential phenomenology which emphasizes the human experience of being-in-the-world of technology, inviting a profound philosophical inquiry into consciousness, moral agency, responsibility, and the potential transformation of human identity. Examining the moral implications of the growing integration of AI into various aspects of human society, this inquiry sought to unravel the existential questions surrounding the ethical dimensions of human-AI interactions while encouraging individuals to critically engage with the essence of technology and recognize its influence on the way we experience and understand our

---

[208] Heidegger, *Being and Time*, 354.

[209] Heidegger, *The Question Concerning Technology and Other Essays*, 35.

existence. Addressing these questions was essential for navigating the ethical and existential implications of advancing artificial intelligence.

References:

COUNCIL OF EUROPE, Recommendation CM/Rec of the Committee of Ministers to member States on developing and promoting digital citizenship education, (2019), 10 https://search.coe.int/cm/Pages/result_details.aspx?ObjectID=090000168098de08

FLORIDI, Lucian, *The Ethics of Artificial Intelligence: Principles, Challenges, and Opportunities.* Oxford: Oxford University Press, 2023.

GERKE, Sara K, MINSSEN Timmo, and COHEN Glenn, "Ethical and legal challenges of artificial intelligence-driven healthcare," *Artificial Intelligence in Healthcare*, (Elsevier 2020), P.295-336. DOI: https://doi.org/10.1016/B978-0-12-818438-7.00012-5

HEIDEGGER, Martin. *Being and Time*, Trans., John Macquarrie & Edward Robinson. New York and London: Harper & Row Publishers, 1962.

_____, *The Question Concerning Technology and Other Essays*, Trans., William Lovitt. New York and London: Garland Publishing, INC., 1977.

HOLMES, Wayne Jen Persson, Irene-Angelica CHOUNTA, Barbara WASSON ,and Vania DIMITROVA, "Artificial Intelligence and Education: A critical view through the lens of human rights, democracy and the rule of law," *Council of Europe*, (November2022), 16. https://rm.coe.int/artificial-intelligence-and-education-a-critical-view-through-the-lens/1680a886bd

MICHELMAN, Stephen, *Historical Dictionary of Existentialism.* Lanham: The Scarecrow Press. Inc, 2008.

RUSSEL, Stuart and Peter NORVIG, *Artificial Intelligence: A Modern Approach*, 3rd Ed. Boston, London: Prentice Hall, 2010.

SCHNEIR, Bruce, *Data and Goliath: The Hidden Battles to Collect your Data and Control Your World.* New York, London: W.W. Norton & Company, 2015.

PART FOUR

AI AND THE ANTHROPOLOGICAL QUESTIONS

Artificial Intelligence and the Question of Artificial Person: Possibility or Hot Air?

Munguci D. Etriga, AJ, holds a PhD in Philosophy, with a focus on Metaphysics and Cosmology. Currently he is the Director of the Institute of Philosophy (IOP) at Tangaza University, and a Part-time Lecturer of Philosophy, at the Apostles of Jesus Institute of Philosophy and Theology (AJIPT), both in Nairobi – Kenya.

Abstract

Today Artificial intelligence (AI) is a non-expendable reality in any discourses and progress of human person. Since its renaissance in 1970s, it has continually presented lots of excitement, expectation and anxiety. Several questions, therefore, abound. The question of person and its corollaries are not excluded. What, for instance, does it mean to be a person? and is artificial person possible? If yes, what nomenclature and dignity does it have? If no, how should humans interact with artificially intelligible objects or systems that exhibit traits synonymous to person? This paper examines these questions. It proceeds from (i) the notion person, to (ii) what it means to be person, to (iii) the possibility of artificial person, and to (iv) how humans ought to interact with artificially intelligent objects. The paper concludes with the claim that the compound term 'artificial-person' is contradictory, nonsensical and hence a hot air.

Key Words: Artificial, Intelligence, Artificial Intelligence, Person, Artificial Person.

Introduction

The most basic philosophical definition of man hitherto is a rational animal. The rationality in question is best depicted by intelligence. Classical metaphysical terms categorize intelligent beings as persons. It is probably for this that today certain manmade objects or systems that depict high degrees of intelligence evoke fears of the possibility of Artificial-Persons. Coincidentally, the theme of the possibility of Artificial-Person upon which my presentation was based on that actual day of the symposium after many symposiasts seemed like the zenith of the discourses. For as so far depicted in most of the antecedent articles in this book, there were engaging debates about Artificial Intelligence and human traits. Issues such as consciousness, free-will, empathy, intentionality, guilt, community, and language were of particular concern so much so that there was a clear impression at the end that the line between AI products like robots and their makers is blurry. In other words, Artificial-Persons and Human-Persons became apparently synonymous. My main thrust in this paper is therefore to debunk any possibilities of such a thing as *Artificial-Person*.

What is 'Person?'

Before delving into the question of artificial-person, I chose to treat the notion 'person'. No universal conception of person exists. There, however, are key elements in myriads of existent conceptions of person that can help in our grasp of the notion. I will highlight these elements from certain anthropological conceptions both Western and African. Ubuntu and Lögbara conceptions of the human person will particularly suffice for the latter.

Etymologically, person is from Greek πρόσωπο (prósopo) for the artificial mask employed to designate a theatre actor. It never at all connoted man or human person. Latin later used the infinitive *personare* "to personify", denoting the role of an actor on a stage.

In Roman law, "person" meant someone who by virtue of a name was recognizable and could play a role in a society with a dignity based on birth, wealth and lineage.[210] This is consonant with the Lögbara conception in which person is only possible in a communitarian context, where blood and soul are the media of linkage.

---

[210] Jose Angel Lombo & Francesco Russo, *Philosophical Anthropology: An Introduction*, Via St. Agostino, Rev. James Socias, Roma, 2017, 151

ARTIFICIAL INTELLIGENCE AND THE QUESTION OF ARTIFICIAL PERSON: POSSIBILITY OR HOT AIR?

In ancient Greece, philosophical discourses focused on man rather than person. Plato, for instance, conceived of man as a universal, eternal, unchangeable and necessary reality. 'This man', 'that man' or an individual man, for him was temporal, accidental and unreal. The real man is a form. In subsequent periods, this came to be identified with the human soul.

Medieval age conceived of person from individuality and divinity centeredness. John Damascene, for instance, defined person as "he who, expressing himself through his own operations, presents a manifestation of himself that distinguishes him from others of the same nature as him."[211] His thought shows the presence of an existential conception of person in classical thought. Richard of Saint Victor would define a human person as "individual or incommunicable existence of a rational nature," and the divine person as "incommunicable existence of divine nature."[212] Besides divinity, incommunicability is thus another key element of person.

Severinus Boethius on his part posited an explicit reference to individuality and rationality through his famous account of person as "an individual substance of a rational nature."[213] Streamlining this in compound terms, Thomas Aquinas later defined person as a *"subsistens rationale"* or that "which subsists in an intellectual or a rational nature."[214] The term *subsistens* in this Thomistic framework encapsulates the three key elements hitherto seen in western conception of person: individual, nature and substance, so that person (corporeal or spiritual), emerges as the most perfect in all nature, that is, a subsistent individual of a rational nature.

Modern times, characterized by crisis in human knowledge conceived of person in terms of thought, consciousness, and existence. Rene Descartes, for instance, delimited human existence to thought in his famous *corgito ergo sum* maxim. David Hume would later conceive of persons not as substances but bundles of perceptions. To John Locke,

---

[211] Jose Angel Lombo & Francesco Russo, p. 156.

[212] Jose Angel Lombo & Francesco Russo, p. 156.

[213] Severenus Boethius, *Liber de persona et duabus naturis contra Eutychen et Nestorium, ad Joannem Diaconum Ecclesiae*, Chapter III, PL 64, 1343.

[214] Thomas Aquinas, *Summa Contra Gentiles*, IV, c. 35; *Summa Theologiae*, III, q. 2, a. 2.

person is a "thinking intelligent being, that has reason and reflection, and can consider itself as itself, the same thinking thing in different times and places; which it does only by that consciousness, which is inseparable from thinking."[215] Thus, while Descartes highlights the element of thought in the understanding of person and Hume perception or understanding, Locke highlights "consciousness, self-consciousness, intelligence, reason and reflection, as well as identity across time and place."[216] The Lockean notion, however, falls short of indicating to what ontological category persons belong. It, for instance, is not explicit as to whether persons are immaterial souls, or human souls, or human beings; neither does it say if persons are embodied or bodies of perceptions. Nonetheless, clearly, person in the modern conception is devoid of any reference to specific entities like organisms, biological beings, or immaterial souls. In the current era of AI, it would mean that any systems or objects exhibiting traits as thought, intelligence, reason and consciousness, are not excluded from the domain of persons.

The Lögbara of North-Western Uganda and North-Eastern Democratic Republic of Congo, till the onset of proselytizing religious enterprises of the 19th Century, seemed not to have had a word for person in their lexicon. The agents of the proselytizing religions, particularly Christianity, adopted *adhia* for person in the Christian sense. Humans, angels and God, all belong here. Primordially, however, the Lögbara lexicon had *bha* exclusively for the human person, *bhandii* for embodied human person, *'bha draapi bho ri* for dead person, *bha bhua* for the dead but the not yet resurrected, inclusive of ghosts; and *ori* for the resurrected human person. Clearly in all these connotations the word *'bha* (person) is paradoxically conceived as a communitarian individual of a spiritual nature, from which God the Divine and other spiritual beings are excluded.[217] Hence, *bha* in the Lögbara anthropology precisely connotes a human nature that is communitarian, individual and spiritual.

---

[215] John Locke, *Essay Concerning Human Understanding*, ed. by W. Carroll, Bristol, Thoemmes, 1990, II, xxvii, p. 9.

[216] John Locke, *Essay Concerning Human Understanding*, p. 43.

[217] Cf. Munguci D. Etriga, *Anthropological Discourse on Person: A Lögbara Metaphysics of the Sociality of Bha – Human Person*, 2024, p. 182. Pending Publication.

Consonant to the Lögbara anthropology, Ubuntu anthropology conceives of person more in terms of the human person. It particularly highlights communitarian nature of person; that one can't exist as a human person in isolation. The key elements of the human person it highlights are: relationality, reciprocity, communion, care, responsibility and hospitality. My humanity, in other words, is caught up and is inextricably bound up in yours, better expressed by the following Mbiti's famous axiom: "I'm because you are; and since we are, therefore I am."[218] Hence, I am person because I belong.

In a nutshell, the notion of 'person' in the myriads of existent anthropological conceptions cited, subsumes the following key elements among others: substance, incommunicability, community, individuality, rationality, spirituality, consciousness, and existence.

What Does it Mean to Be Person?

What then precisely is the meaning of substance, individuality, rationality, spirituality, consciousness, existence and community as elements of person? This is what is addressed under this theme. The purpose is to establish the basis for the determination of whether manmade objects exhibiting certain degrees of intelligence as is the case with robotics and automatons, hence, finite objects, can be persons or not. For this reason, my treatment is limited to the meaning of the elements in question as found in persons of finite nature. Human persons will, particularly, be examined. God, angels, or other intelligent persons are excluded.

To begin with, to be a person means to subsist. To subsist is to have an own act of existence. Hence, a person has an own act of existence. Persons do not inhere in something else but subsist in themselves. This connotes that I or you as persons need not to inhere in something or somebody else. We are substances. An unborn baby is not excluded. It has its own act of existence really distinct from the mother's. Therefore, whether unborn, adult, or an angel, to be person is to subsist.

A chief characteristic of this subsistence is its incommunicability. Persons of finite nature have their own "undonatable" acts of existence.

---

[218] Mbiti, J. S., *African Religions and Philosophies*. Oxford: Heinemann, 1970, p. 141.

In other words, their existence cannot be rented, borrowed or donated. Even in the cases of cloning or organ transplant, one's act of existence as a person is incommunicable.[219] Such a subsistence is rendered effective only through an entitative act, that is, the first act that brings a finite person into existence. It moves a finite person from non-being to being, with the immaterial dimension henceforth remaining devoid of non-existence.

To be a person is to be an individual. Individuality is absence of shared identity. And identity is a lack of sameness or similarity. Hence, being a person is to lack sameness or similarity with another. Every person, that is to say, is one in themselves but distinct from others. This bestows a unique character of identity to persons in which one as a person is an individual entity identical to itself or separate from others. It renders a person unrepeatable, un-multipliable, never doubled and indeed never replicable or carbon-capable. As previously alluded to, the principle responsible for this kind of individuality is incommunicable. Accordingly, it is only to the nature of persons that a unique form of individuality belongs.[220] No other beings, natural or artificial, partake in this individuality.

To be an individual who is a person is to be a whole or complete. This, however, should not be construed in quantitative or logical terms. The wholeness or completeness in question connotes the richness of one's act of being. To be a person, hence, is to be a complete being or reality. There is no such thing as half or incomplete person. Similarly, a person is not just a part with respect to a whole. Soren Kierkegaard's following paradoxical terms bring this better: "A thousand men are less than one man."[221] There is nothing in reality like "a thousand men" but "this man," and "that man," each of which is a whole or complete. Denis, for instance, is not a person because he is a man (a universal

---

[219] Even if we could precisely reproduce the bodily characteristics of a person, we would not have the same person because he is an individual who exists in his own original and unrepeatable singularity. Cf. J.F Crosby, *The Selfhood of the Human Person*, Washington, D.C.: The Catholic University of America Press, 1996, pp. 43-44, 52-53.

[220] Cf. Thomas Aquinas, *Summa Theologiae*, I, q.29, a.1.

[221] Cf. Soren Kierkegaard, *Diario* (1847-1848), Brescia: Morcelliana, 1980, Vol. 4, IX A 91, n. 1791.

being) or he is a group of rational animals. He is a person because he is "this man" or "that man".

Being a person means being rational. Any entity termed person by nature possess the capacity to cognitively assimilate everything existent and apprehend the intelligibility, beauty, and goodness of existence. This is notwithstanding the question as to whether such inherent capacity is partially or fully realizable subject to other factors. Hence, as a rational entity, a person has the inherent capacity to know the surrounding world and to extract universal concepts therefrom.

To be a person is to possess a spiritual nature. It means one is endowed with consciousness and able to overcome limitations of space and time. In the Lögbara anthropology, the spiritual nature means a person is not just the body in origin, being, and destiny. It means while the bodily aspect is temporal, the non-bodily is eternal, whose corporeal nature only begun in time.

Being a person means being free. The main feature of this freedom is the capacity to have self-determination and self-control. With regard to finite persons, freedom is the capacity to determine one's own course of action within the finite nature of existence. This freedom is the basis on which personal acts: thinking, loving, charity, forgiveness, appreciation, moral acts, etc. are rooted. Individuals other than persons: natural (brutes, plants, stone, etc.), or artificial (computers, robots, automatons, etc.) can, through training or programming, perform these acts but only in as far as they are manipulated to do so. In and by themselves these objects or systems are incapable of such personal acts rooted in free will.

The corollary of freedom is responsibility. To be person means to be responsible. For, just as freedom is a fundamental element of the human person, responsibility is, because it is always an appeal to freedom. Kant highlights this better in his autonomy of the will which is the solid foundation of the moral law. It remains to be seen if AI objects like robots are capable of acting responsibly as a manifestation of their own free will.

Consequent to freedom and responsibility, to be person means to be capable and liable to doing evil. This is not to highlight that persons (human, angelic, or divine) are naturally evil. Rather it highlights the inherent capacity to make wrong choices. The basis of this is the capacity for free-will and self-determination. It means that in the pursuit of self-fulfillment, persons, especially of the finite nature, are capable of acting evil.

As alluded to above, to be person is to have an inherent capacity for self-fulfillment. This is an existential self-striving in persons, particularly in the finite persons, towards self-attainment. In the human domain, this striving entails various physical-biological developments comprising the entire person both in its corporeal and spiritual dimensions. This capacity for self-fulfillment renders the human person an open project without implying incompleteness as an individual.

The inherent capacity for self-fulfillment as finite persons leads to constant self-transcendence. Persons, though may happen to have corporeal nature as is the case with humans, have the ability to transcend the limitations of corporeality and move outside that domain. Hence, humans as finite persons as they may be, constantly seek to project themselves beyond their particular situations. Pascal puts it better: "Man infinitely transcends man."[222] Human persons discover deep in themselves the instinct towards goodness, towards truth and towards beauty.

To be a person is to be capable of establishing relationships. It means in transcending oneself (self-transcendence), a person is able to have a relationship not only with the self but also with the other, that is, other persons (people, intelligible beings of the second mode of existence, or God). In Lögbara metaphysics of the sociality of *bha*, one is inherently relational right from conception through the medium of blood and soul as seen bellow in the communitarian bondage.

To be a person is to be communitarian. This communitarianism issues from the relational nature of person. Both the Ubuntu and Lögbara anthropologies explicate this clearly. In the case of the later, it is spelt out that the communitarian nature stems right at fertilization with regards to *bha*. The parents through the medium of blood link the newly conceived to the community both of the living and the dead (non-living), while the medium of soul links the new person to the spiritual (divine) community. This communitarian bondage is unbreakable, even

---

[222] B. Pascal, *Pensees*, Paris: Cerf, 1982, 371; cf. *Pensees*, 369.

if it may physically seem so through death or long distances. It is an indelible communal relationship with no expiry date.

In spite of being communitarian, being a person means having an autonomous existence. A person acts not only in accordance with the dictates of community and natural instincts to achieve their ends or destiny. They also deliberately employ these dictates, knowing their purpose to direct the course of their lives. This deliberation is in one's sovereignty despite their communitarian bondage.

Being a person means having an inherent value. It means one as a person is an end unto himself and never simply a means. He is a means that exists *per se* and cannot be used as a mere instrument subordinated to other ends.[223] Such a value is never acquired or merited. Thus, any actions or projects that place man in-between the actor and end as a means do violence to what a person is.

The inherent value in a person renders him/her in possession of an inalienable dignity. This is a dignity that cannot be taken away, donated, or assumed by another because each one possesses his/her own ontological identity as a person. This is the ontological basis that separates a person from a mere *thing*. It is an entirely different rank and dignity in Derridean terms.[224]

To be a person means having an inherent desire for happiness. The self-transcendence project in human persons towards goodness, truth and beauty has happiness as its goal. Accordingly, to be a finite person is to have inherent desire for happiness. Such a desire is insatiable in temporality of existence. In humans and indeed in all finite intelligences, the desire for happiness is the basis for eternity in their finitude.

Clearly, therefore, to be a person, especially of finite nature, like human, means to be characterized by subsistence, incommunicability, individuality, and wholeness. Such an existent is equally capable of exercising rationality, freedom, responsibility, act evil, feel pain, and seek self-fulfillment. In so doing, the entity termed person must be capable of self-transcendence, establishment of relationships, and be

---

[223] Cf. I. Kant, *Fondazione della metafisica dei costume*, Milan: Rusconi, 1994, section II, pp. 141-145.
[224] J. Derrida, *The Animal That Therefore I Am*, David Wills (trans.), New York: Fordham University Press, 2008, pp. 92-93.

communitarian yet autonomous. Above all, to be a person is to possess an inherent value, inalienable dignity, and an intrinsic desire for happiness.

Is Artificial Person Possible?

Having established what it means to be person, I now turn to the fundamental question of the paper: Is artificial person possible? By 'artificial' I mean what is man-made or produced by a human being as opposed to natural. It is a product of the human reason, particularly that which is a copy of something natural. Thus, while I take the 'natural' as "that which is and acts from its own internal principle, [the] artificial is that which is or acts from an external principle."[225] Accordingly, 'artificial person', as a matter of definition, is a manmade person. From the precedent discourse, it is clear what elements characterize person. In order to respond to the question as to whether artificial-person is possible, we shall therefore inquire if these characteristic elements in question can singularly or collectively be appropriated to manmade objects or systems like robotics or automatons.

To begin with, we ask ourselves if a human product subsists or can be a substance. To be a substance as previously seen is to have an own act of existence. We thus ask whether a robot, for instance, has an own act of existence. Certainly, every existent, including robots serving in a hotel, hospital, bank, or doing some Samantha services subsist. However, first, it should be noted that while robots have forms, their forms as principles of the act of existence do not self-exist.

> *The soul of irrational beings does not have existence of itself, but thanks to it an individual comes into being. [...] its function is limited to conforming the body and enabling it to undertake the bodily actions specific to the species.*[226]

Contrarily, the human soul does not only conform and enable the body to undertake actions specific to the human species. It equally

---

[225] Congiunti L., *Philosophy: Outlines of Philosophy of Nature*, Urbaniana University Press, 2020, p. 133.

[226] Jose Angel Lombo & Francesco Russo, *Philosophical Anthropology: An Introduction*, p. 135.

ARTIFICIAL INTELLIGENCE AND THE QUESTION OF ARTIFICIAL PERSON: POSSIBILITY OR HOT AIR?

possesses a perfection that surpasses the properties of hylomorphism. This renders the human person capable of engaging in actions shared by beings of intelligent and divine natures. For this reason, the origin, and hence, nature, of the human form or soul cannot be accounted for on the basis of corporeality. Again, since existence does not belong to corporeal nature and humans have a nature that transcends corporeality, it follows that they are capable of having an existence of their own, for which their origin can be accounted. Manmade products, to which those exhibiting some degree of intelligence belong, are excluded from this category of self-existence.

In their category of existence different from person's that self-exist, artificial bodies: robots, automatons, computers, 'artificial persons', etc., do not possess the unity of natural bodies that would render them exist as individuals. Theirs is more of aggregates of individuals or substances. Strictly put, artificial bodies are not really individuals as persons are:

> *Artificial bodies do not possess the unity of the natural bodies; in fact, they act as aggregations of parts, put together by deep – chemical, dynamic, electronic ... - but nevertheless extrinsic bonds. Artificial objects are not really individuals, as they are not indivisible in themselves, but if anything, they present themselves as systems of individuals, and individual elements are often traceable at every low level (even as molecules or atoms).*[227]

To be a person is to be an individual that renders one identical to oneself. And since artificial objects cannot be individuals, 'artificial persons' are incapable of existing as persons.

Corollary to self-existence, the human substance is of incommunicable nature. It is undonatable or unsharable. Accordingly, robots, computers, or automatons (manmade products exhibiting some degree of intelligence) do not have own acts of existence, for which they are not substances, or they have own acts of existence which are donatable, for which they are not characteristic of persons. "Artificial objects", as previously alluded to, "have a substantiality in that they subsist in being, but precisely as a group of substances and not as

---

[227] Congiunti L., *Philosophy: Outlines of Philosophy of Nature*, p. 134.

individuals."[228] It is for this that their existence is communicable. Two or more robots, for instance, can, in real time, be designed or programmed to have same existence and modes of operation, precisely for this type of existence. Such robots can be fed or programmed to exist and collapse at the same time because they share same act of existence. Due to this sharing of the act of existence, these (two or more) robots can collectively collapse as one entity. Persons can never collapse or die collectively as one entity. Each person though may be forced to collapse by same factor, does so individually. In other words, every individual person has their own death or collapse. It therefore means that the act of existence possessed by artificial objects or systems must be of another category or degree different from person's act of existence. Person's act of existence is unsharable and undonatable. Hence, artificial objects or systems to which 'artificial persons' belong cannot be persons.

Can a robot be an individual? It emerged in the previous submission that to be individual is to be identical to self. Can a human product be identical to itself? There definitely is no question about the identity of a computer or robot. Every computer, robot, automaton, or Samantha is identical to itself. Nonetheless, whereas two or more computers as seen above can quantitatively, qualitatively, and existentially be identical in every aspect, persons are incapable of such. No persons are quantitatively, qualitatively, and existentially identical in real-time. Each person is an individual or is identical to him/herself. What this means is that every person is incapable of not being identical to him/herself. Hence, artificial objects or systems like computers or robots that exhibit traits similar to persons are incapable of being persons.

Can a human product be rational or intelligent? In other words, can there be artificial rationality or intelligence? Rationality is an essential accident of form that concerns the capacity to cognitively assimilate reality and apprehend the intelligibility of existence. Being rational, in other words, is being able to know the surrounding world and extract universal concepts therefrom. No robot or computer has an inherent capacity for intellection and mastery of its actions beyond its programming. While in certain instances computers may become rogue, thus seeming to demonstrate that they have gone beyond their

---

[228] Congiunti L., *Philosophy: Outlines of Philosophy of Nature*, p. 134.

programming, it is only that the programmer in question fails to exhaustively understand the limits or extent to which its intended programme goes. This in essence only means that the 'rogue' action is beyond the programmer's limited knowledge at the time of programming but not beyond the programmer's programme. Hence, even the most intelligent computers or robots do act in as far as they are fed to do so by human rationality. The actions of robots or computers never arise out of intelligence that depicts the cognitive capacity to freely assimilate and apprehend the intelligibility, beauty, and goodness of surroundings and actions. Too, if rationality or intelligence connotes such inherent cognitive capacity of freedom to master actions, then the concept of 'artificial intelligence' in its entirety is not intelligent. There, simply, is no artificial intelligence or rationality. Manmade objects, accordingly, are incapable of intelligence.

To be person means to be free. The main feature of this freedom is the intrinsic capacity to have self-determination and self-control, so that persons are able to act morally. Do machines, systems, etc. have the freedom arising out of free will to act morally? Machines or systems can only act as if they are moral. But the truth is no machine or system is a moral agent. Machines by nature are amoral. Even unmanned aerial war machines, like any other guns, are never moral agents to act moral or immoral as persons in principle do. For all manmade machines in and by themselves are devoid of free will, hence incapable of being persons. The so-called artificial intelligence that defines artificial person is not excluded.

To be person is to act responsibly. No manmade machine acts responsibly unless programmed to execute certain acts that can be termed responsible acts. Currently efforts are in progress for production of robotic systems controlled by chips having the capacity to be fed with emotions. Effectively, these will be able to empathize and respond accordingly in given situations and needs. Automated vehicles, for instance, that not only read and interpret traffic rules, but avoid accidents are in service today. Watching robotic machines diligently serving customers in restaurants or operating patients in highly computerized hospitals leave one with owe not only at the efficiency of these systems but the carefulness and responsibility exhibited. Nonetheless, in such cases still, the responsibility in question is not essence of the machines but rather their programmers.

ISSUES IN ARTIFICIAL INTELLIGENCE:
A PHILOSOPHICAL INTERROGATION

To be a person means to be capable and liable of doing evil, that is, persons have the inherent capacity to willfully make wrong choices. No robot or computer is capable of doing evil in and by itself. Machines are devoid of the requisite elements for moral judgment. Moral evil is outside the domain of artificial objects that exhibit certain degrees of intelligence. The capacity for morally praiseworthy or blameworthy acts is an exclusive reserve of persons. Hence, no being, object, or system liable to good or evil acts belongs to the nomenclature of persons. Robotic objects or systems that depict certain degrees of intelligence are not and cannot be persons.

To be a person means to be able to encounter the reality of pain; pain as an object of senses and intellect. While highly automated machines today have the capacity to sense, interpret, and react accordingly, that however, is possible only insofar as their programming goes. Such a programming is devoid of the intrinsic mastery over pain, whether self or other. There, however, is the common argument that machines in DMC (Dangerous Mechanical Conditions) that easily are detected by unnecessary sounds produced feel pain; and indeed, today certain machines programmed by chips are capable of expressing feelings of pain. As hinted elsewhere, these, nonetheless are only in as far as the interpretation of their conditions (like the noise they make) and their programming is concerned. Any entity termed person is capable of pain: sensitive or intellective. Robotic objects or systems that depict certain degrees of intelligence are not and cannot feel this pain. They, therefore, are excluded from the nomenclature of entities termed persons.

To be a person is to have an autonomous existence. It means persons, particularly of the human nature, have the capacity to use their natural instincts, knowing their purpose, to consciously direct the course of their life. While manmade objects or systems may have autonomous existence from their makers and beings other than themselves, these objects or systems are incapable of consciously directing the course of their actions towards a *telos*. It is the maker that defines any machine's *telos* and directions towards it. Any person of the finite nature has this inherently conscious *telos*. Since robotic objects or systems that depict certain degrees of intelligence are not and cannot consciously self-direct towards a telos, they are not party to the category of persons.

ARTIFICIAL INTELLIGENCE AND THE QUESTION OF ARTIFICIAL PERSON: POSSIBILITY OR HOT AIR?

To be a person is to be communitarian - a bondage that's unbreakable. Machines, systems or a group of robots can be grouped together. However, such a group never constitutes a community. It lacks common aspirations, purposes and shared values. While a group of robots or automatons are often grouped to achieve certain purposes, it is not their purpose. The purpose or goal in question is of their makers or assemblers. Persons of any modes or species have common aspirations, purposes and values that set them as a community. This is despite the reality of divergences due to individuality and autonomy. A person, and particularly of the human nature, is communitarian by definition. The Ubuntu and Lögbara anthropologies previously highlighted make this more lucid. Robotic objects or systems that depict certain degrees of intelligence are excluded from this human privilege. Certain beings other than persons, however, can come close to this communitarian nature but only so, as social beings.

To be a person is to have an inherent value that cannot be subordinated to any other end of finite essence. A finite person, though of a finite nature, has no finite end other than itself to which it is subordinated. The human person, for instance, is an end in itself. Machines or systems, inclusive of those exhibiting high degrees of intelligence, are instruments designed by the human person for the achievement of his own self-fulfillment. This, however, is notwithstanding abuses of these machines or systems. To be noted, too, is that since robotic objects or systems that depict certain degrees of intelligence are excluded from such inherent values, they cannot belong to the nomenclature of persons.

Being a person means having an inalienable dignity that cannot be taken away, donated, or assumed by another because each one possesses his/her own ontological identity as a person. Machines or robots can be made, unmade, destroyed, or reprogrammed. Even though today some persons may seem to have more affinity, affection, and high regard for their machines, this in no way turns the machines in question to possessing inalienable dignity. They are mere *things*. Robots or automatons are included in this list, hence excluded from the category of persons.

Being a person means having the inherent capacity for self-transcendence. Machines, robots, or automatons lack the capacity to self-transcend. They lack the self-consciousness to enable them to transcend the limitations of temporality. For this reason, it is not possible to talk of Artificial persons.

Human self-transcend towards goodness, truth, and beauty for attainment of happiness, is in turn, the basis of the desire for eternity. Robots, automatons, and systems, for what we know, are incapable of existential striving for eternity. All persons of finite nature have this inherent and insatiable character as part of their definition. Objects or systems exhibiting traits similar to persons never strive for eternity, and hence are incapable of being persons.

In sum, the notion *Artificial-person*, whose construct is premised on attributes of some purported manmade persons, is illusory. For the entity termed person must essentially and inherently possess the previously subsumed elements of a person. These elements collectively belie the construct that a person can never be artificial, hence, not manmade. The naturalness of a person renders it original, inherently valuable, highly dignified, and of purposeful existence not donated, approved, or ascribed by a being of finite nature. Such, therefore, renders any constructs of artificial-person merely premised on purported artificial intelligence a hot air.

How Should Humans Interact with Objects or Systems Exhibiting Traits Similar to Persons?

The impossibility and absurdity of Artificial-Person constructed on the basis of the so-called Artificial Intelligence should not, nonetheless, be construed that manmade objects or systems exhibiting certain degrees of intelligence are unreal. The reality of robotic machines and systems that have continued to amaze us, their makers, cannot be denied. Today, for instance, manmade machines decently assist in toilet services while simultaneously monitoring one's health status through urine, stool, pressure, internal organs, blood group, etc. Again, today one can be treated for cancer from Beijing while in Rome, Kampala, or Rio de Genario. Think, for instance, of virtual assistants like Siri and Lexa, personalized content recommendations on streaming platforms, fraud detections in banking, navigation apps that suggest the best routes based on real-time traffic data, or AI apps commonly

ARTIFICIAL INTELLIGENCE AND THE QUESTION OF ARTIFICIAL PERSON: POSSIBILITY OR HOT AIR?

available in smartphones, of computers that render complex tasks otherwise in ordinary ways easy, etc. These indeed are not only exciting developments but have also increasingly become non-expendables in human progress today.

These realities consequently leave us with the question of how we ought to interact with them. Through these objects or systems, it is important, first of all, to appreciate the significant role our own intelligence brings forth in the name of AI. It is, doubtless to say, that devoid of human intelligence, the so-called AI is non-existent. Hence, the known, the unknown, and the unintended outcomes that often make these objects termed rogue in their actions notwithstanding, AI objects deserve to be appreciated as a reflection of human intelligence.

Humans need to monitor, master, and subdue their products. Conscious that no human product is beyond its own mastery, even when for a short while that might seem so, man should seek to master and subdue his own products. Aristotle's centuries-old metaphysical dictum that an effect can only at most be equivalent to what the cause has is relevant in this regard. It would therefore be unintelligent and detrimental for human intelligence to come with products it cannot afford to subdue.

With the self-knowledge man has regarding his inalienable dignity and inherent value as an end in itself, humans ought to never sell out this naturally endowed nomenclature. Humans only partake in that nomenclature with intelligible beings belonging to a domain in which they are at the base. No other being below them in the hierarchy of existents is a member. Hence, it would be tantamount to abuse of man's dignity, nomenclature, and vocation as persons to place other beings, to speak less of their own products in a position above them.

It is incumbent upon man in his interactions with the so-called AI and its objects or systems to render them transparent and explainable. This is to help their users understand how and why they work and what their limitations and uncertainties are. AI should not be discreet, shrouded in fear and estrangement.

As the author of AI objects or systems, humans have the onus of ensuring that these objects or systems are responsive and adaptive. This is to render them easily adjustable to the user's needs, preferences, goals, and feedback.

Humans should be in position to employ appropriate methods and metrics to evaluate AI objects or systems and their impact on users, society, and the environment. The safety, future, and purpose of the maker and user of AI services should be a priority. Besides, the larger society with all its components must be brought into the picture while humans interact with these objects and systems. It would, for instance, be self-defeating for humans to employ AI products as battle robotic drones that carry out indiscriminate battle-field operations. Any designs of AI systems should ultimately be human, societal, and environmentally friendly.

While AI objects and systems can assist humans in making decisions by providing data-driven insights and improve efficiency and man's quality of existence, their makers need to keep to mind that their use cannot replace human judgment. Humans are still and will always remain non-expendables in decision-making, creativity, and empathy. AI objects and systems only amplify and augment their makers rather than displacing their abilities.

The main objective of human-AI interaction is to create AI systems that are user-friendly, trustworthy, ethical, and beneficial to humans. The capacity and efficiency of AI systems to perform tasks such as understanding natural language, recognizing images, making decisions, algorithmic usages, and learning from data among many are all to the benefit of man.

Conclusion

The article has examined AI and the question of person with specific reference to the human person. While on the one hand the article conceives the 'artificial' as a manmade product that is opposed to the natural or that which is and acts from an external principle, on the other hand, the 'natural' is conceived as that which is and acts from its own internal principle. It has also been established that 'intelligence' is the innate capacity to cognitive and conscious mastery of reality. On these bases, AI is thus defined as any object or system constructed by man exhibiting characteristics of intelligence principally as a copy of human intelligence. And as a corollary to this conception, the article concludes that 'artificial person', as a matter of definition, is a manmade object or system depicting characteristic elements of a person.

The fleeting survey of anthropological conceptions in the first part of the article subsumes person as a reality characterized by common elements such as subsistence, intelligence, incommunicability, individuality, wholeness, community, relatedness, autonomy, consciousness, freedom, responsibility, moral action, empathy, pain, and self-transcendence. Examining the meaning of person, and as to whether AI objects can be persons in the second and third parts, the article fundamentally contends that since intelligence as a mark of rationality in the human person connotes the innate capacity to cognitively and consciously assimilate anything existent and apprehend its intelligibility through universal concepts like beauty, goodness, unity, happiness, etc., no manmade product is capable of such a capacity. Only man, among finite corporeal nature, possesses this innate capacity. He can render intelligible the surrounding world and extract universal concepts therefrom. Intelligence and artificiality are incompatible terms.

Therefore, to be person is to partake in a noble nomenclature proper to intelligent beings. The so-called Artificial-Intelligence or manmade objects that depict certain degrees of intelligence are incapable of intelligence and so excluded from the nomenclature of persons. Any object or system so termed is only so in analogically attributive sense - a resemblance of intelligence devoid of the inborn capacity realizable through cognitive mastery and consciousness. It is the conclusion of the article that the concept of artificial-intelligence belies any prospects for possibility of artificial-person. This should not, however, be construed as a denial of objects or systems like robotics and automatons that exhibit characteristics similar to intelligence. These are real and moreover non-expendables today. Indeed, no serious human discourses and progress is possible today devoid of these systems or objects. The only thing needed is for humans to design and define how to interact with these objects or systems for rendering them more relevant, better, and suitable for the improvement of man's quality of life and his environment. After all, man remains the author and end of any AI objects and systems.

References:

AGOSTINO, *La speranza*, Rome: Citta Nuova, 2002.

ALICI L., *L'altro nell'io:In dialogo con Agostino*, Rome: Citta Nuova, 1999.

ALVIRA T., L. CLAVELL, and T. MALENDO, *Metaphysics*, Manila: Sinag-Tala, 1991.

ARTIGAS M., and J.J. SANGUINETTI, *Filosofia della natura*, Florence: Le Monnier, 1989.

BOETHIUS S., *The theological Tractates*, London, Cambridge: Heinemann Press, 1953.

CONGIUNTI L., *Philosophy: Outlines of Philosophy of Nature*, Urbaniana University Press, 2020.

DERRIDA J., *The Animal That Therefore I Am*, David Wills (trans.), New York: Fordham University Press, 2008.

DESCARTES, R., *I principi della filosofia*, Pars prima, Torino: Bollati Boringhieri, 1992.

EINAR DUENGER Bohn, "Ex Machina: Is Ava a Person?" in *Minding the Future: Artificial Intelligence, Philosophical Visions and Science Fiction*, B. Daiton & A. Tanyi (eds) https://www.researchgate.net/publication/354246027_Ex_Machina_Is_Ava_a_Person

KIERKEGAARD Soren, *Diario*, Brascia: Morcettiana, 1980.

LOCKE, John, *Essay Concerning Human Understanding*. W. Caroll, Bristol, Theommes (eds): Place of Publication & Publisher, 1990

LOMBO, Jose Angel & Francesco RUSSO, *Philosophical Anthropology: An Introduction*. Roma: Year of Publication, 2017.

HEIDEGGER, M., *Being and Time*, New York, Illinois: Harper & Row, 1962.

LEVINAS E., *Humanism of the Other*, Chicago: University of Illinois Press, 2003.

MBITI, J. S., *African Religions and Philosophies*. Oxford: Heinemann, 1970.

MONDIN B., *Philosophical Anthropology: Man – An Impossible Project?*, Rome: Urbaniana University Press, 1985.

MUNGUCI D. Etriga, *Anthropological Discourse on Person: A Lögbara Metaphysics of the Sociality of Bha – Human Person*, 2024. (Unpublished).

ARTIFICIAL INTELLIGENCE AND THE QUESTION OF ARTIFICIAL PERSON: POSSIBILITY OR HOT AIR?

SEVERINUS Boethius, *Liber de Persona et Deabus Naturis Contra Eutychen et Nestorium, ad Joannem Diaconum Ecclesiae*. Pl. 64m 1343.

THOMAS AQUINAS, *Entity and Essence*, Silvano Barruso (trans.), Nairobi: Consolata Institute of Philosophy Press, 2001.

_____, *On Being and Essence*, Armand Maurer (trans.), The Pontifical Institute of Medieval Studies, Toronto: Universa – Wetteren, 1968.

_____, *Summa Contra Gentiles*, Notre Dame, IN-London: University of Notre Dame Press, 1975.

_____, *On Spiritual Creatures*, Milwaukee: Marquette University Press, 1949.

_____, *Summa Theologiae*, London – New York: Blackfriars Publications, 1964.

WOJTYLA K., "The Acting Person", in *The Yearbook of Phenomenological Research10*: Dordrecht, D. Reidel, 1979.

INDEX

Preface and Acknowledgments 7
Introduction 11

PART ONE:
THE PHILOSOPHICAL ANTECEDENTS OF THE AI TECHNOLOGY .. 19

The Philosophical Roots of the
Generative Pre-Trained Transformer Chatterbots 21
Phenomenology of Human Subjectivity in the Hi-Tech Rationality 41

PART TWO: I AND THE EPISTEMOLOGICAL QUESTIONS 73

A Critical Evaluation of Lonergan's Concept of
Human Understanding and Artificial Intelligence (AI) 75
The Abyss between Human and Artificial Intelligence 89

PART THREE: I AND THE MORAL QUESTIONS 101

AI and Free Will Critical Perspectives Based on
Saint Thomas Aquinas' Concept of *Liberum Arbitrium* 103
An Evaluation of the Philosophy of Artificial Intelligence (*AI*)
Through the Lens of Kantian Notion of Freewill 119
Human-Artificial Intelligence Relationship a Moral Inquiry
from a Heideggerian Perspective 139

PART FOUR: I AND THE ANTHROPOLOGICAL QUESTIONS 155

Artificial Intelligence and the Question of Artificial Person:
Possibility or Hot Air? 157

DOMUNI-PRESS
publishing house of DOMUNI Universitas

« Le livre grandit avec le lecteur »
"The book grows with the reader."

Domuni Universitas

Domuni Universitas was founded in 1999 by French Dominicans. It offers Bachelor, Master and Doctorate degrees by distance learning, as well as "à la carte" (stand-alone) courses and certificates in philosophy, theology, religious sciences, and social sciences. It welcomes several thousand students on its teaching platform, which operates in five languages: French, English, Spanish, Italian, and Arabic. The platform is accompanied by more than three hundred professors and tutors. Anchored in the Order of Preachers, Domuni Universitas benefits from its centuries-old tradition of study and research. Innovative in many ways, Domuni consists of an international network that offers courses to students worldwide.

To find out more about Domuni:
www.domuni.eu

DOMUNI-PRESS
publishing house of DOMUNI Universitas

« Le livre grandit avec le lecteur »
"The book grows with the reader."

The publishing house

Domuni-Press disseminates research and publishes works in the academic fields of interest of Domuni Universitas: theology, philosophy, spirituality, history, religions, law and social sciences. Domuni-Press is part of a lively research community located at the heart of the Dominican network. Domuni-Press aims to bring readers closer to their texts by making it possible, via the help of today's digital technology, to have immediate access to them, while ensuring a quality paperback edition. Each work is published in both forms. The key word is simplicity. The subjects are approached with a clear editorial line: academic quality, accessible to all, with the aim of spreading the richness of Christian thought. Six collections are available: theology, philosophy, spirituality, Bible, history, law and social sciences. Domuni-Press has its own online bookshop: www.domunipress.fr. Its books are also available on its main distance selling website: Amazon, Fnac.com, and in more than 900 bookshops and sales outlets around the world.

To find out more about the publishing house:
www.domunipress.fr

EXTRACT FROM THE CATALOGUE

Jean-François ARNOUX,
   Et le désert refleurira.

Sabine GINALHAC,
   Désir d'enfant. L'éclairage inattendu des récits bibliques.

Pierrette FUZAT,
   Un nom au bout de la nuit. Le combat de Jacob.

Patrice SABATER,
   La terre en Palestine/Israël.

Marie MONNET,
   Emmanuel Levinas. La relation à l'autre.

Apollinaire KIVYAMUNDA,
   Maurice Zundel, une biographie spirituelle.

Juliette BORDES,
   Viens Colombe. Saint Jean de la Croix.

Joseph MARTY,
   Christianisme et Cinéma.

Michel VAN AERDE,
   Le père retrouvé

Monique-Lise COHEN, Marie-Thérèse DESOUCHE,
   Emmanuel Levinas et la pensée de l'infini.

Claire REGGIO,
   Le christianisme des premiers siècles.

Ameer JAJE,
   Diaconesses. Les femmes dans l'Église syriaque.

Jean-Paul COUJOU (sous la direction de),
   L'État et le pouvoir.

Françoise DUBOST,
   L'Évangile des animaux.

Markus JOST,
La Bible à l'école d'Ignace de Loyola et de Menno Simons.

Paul TAVARDON, ocso,
Trappistes en terre sainte. Des moines au cœur de la géopolitique. Latroun, 1890-1946 (T.1).

Paul TAVARDON, ocso,
Trappistes en terre sainte. Des moines au cœur de la géopolitique. Latroun, 1946-1991 (T.2).

Marie MONNET (sous la direction de),
La source théologique du droit.

Nilson Léal DE SA,
La vie fraternelle.

Apollinaire KIVYAMUNDA,
Maurice Zundel. La relation à Dieu.

Lara LOYE,
Fraternités.

Bernadette ESCAFFRE,
Vocations. Quand Dieu appelle.

Raphaël HAAS,
Pleine conscience. Bouddhisme et christianisme en dialogue.

Augustin WILIWOLI,
Axel Honneth. Lutter pour la reconnaissance.

Louis FROUART,
Pascal. Cœur, Corps, Esprit.

Emmanuel BOISSIEU,
Platon. Une manière de vivre.

Emmanuel BOISSIEU,
Kant. Une philosophie de la liberté.

Marie MONNET,
Dieu migrant.

Thérèse HEBBELINCK,
L'Église catholique et les juifs (T.1 et T.2).

Béatrice PAPASOGLOU,
Qu'est-ce que l'homme ?

Augustin WILIWOLI SIBILONI op,
Ce que les philosophes disent du vivre-ensemble.

François MENAGER,
Yves Bonnefoy, poète et philosophe.

Nicole AWAIS,
L'art d'enseigner le fait religieux.

Thérèse M. ANDREVON,
Une théologie à la frontière (T.1 et T2).

Michel VAN AERDE,
Venez vous reposer. Antidotes spirituels au burn-out.

Agnès GODEFROY,
Bien vieillir, dans les pas d'Abraham.

Olivier BELLEIL,
Résolution des conflits dans l'Église primitive.

Anton MILH op & Stephan VAN ERP,
Identité et visibilité. Conflits de générations chez les Dominicains.

Denis LABOURE,
Astrologie et religion au Moyen Âge.

Jorel FRANÇOIS,
Voltaire, philosophe de la religion.

Augustin WILIWOLI SIBILONI op,
La reconnaissance. Réparer les blessures.

Jean Baptiste ZEKE,
Loi naturelle et post-humanisme.

Emmanuel BOISSIEU,
Paul Ricœur. Un inconditionnel de l'amour.

Ameer JAJE,
Le chiisme. Clés historiques et théologiques.

Jean-René PEGGARY,
L'aube d'une pensée américaine. L'individu chez H. D. Thoreau.

Jean-François ARNOUX,
Comme un feu dévorant. Flammèches d'une lecture incarnée de la Bible.

Olivier BELLEIL,
L'autre dans l'islam coranique.

Sœur Agnès DE LA CROIX,
Miroir juif des évangiles.

Jean-Michel COSSE,
Au centre de l'âme.

Jean-Paul BALDAZZA,
Antoine. Un saint d'Orient et d'Occident.

Ameer JAJE,
Marie dans l'islam.

Olivier PERRU,
Le corps malade.

Jesmond MICALLEF,
Trinitarian Ontology.

Abel TOE,
Pauvreté et développement au Burkina Faso.

Jude Thaddeus MBI AKEM,
Le développement en Afrique.

Claude LICHTERT,
Lire la Bible ensemble.

Jorel FRANÇOIS,
Voltaire, philosophe contre le fanatisme.

Bruno CALLEBAUT,
Les Évangiles. Leurs origines, leurs exégèses.

Claude LICHTERT,
La parole pour sortir de soi. Dieu et les humains aujourd'hui : parcours biblique.

Heriberto CABRERA REYES,
Effondrement, apocalypse ou renaissance ? Théologie en temps de crise.

Patrick MONJOU,
Comment prêcher à la fin du Moyen Âge ? (T. 1 et T. 2).

Robert PLÉTY,
À la découverte du Rabbi de Nazareth (T. 1).

Robert PLÉTY,
À la rencontre du Rabbi de Nazareth (T. 2).

Jules KATSURANA,
Guide pour la Prévention de la violence sexiste.

Jacques FOURNIER,
La Trinité, mystère d'amour.

Louis D'HÉROUVILLE,
Marie-Madeleine, femme pascale.

Olivier PERRU,
Martin-Stanislas Gillet (1875-1951). La peur de l'effort intellectuel.

Paul-Marcel LEMAIRE,
Vivre l'Évangile.

John Jack LYNCH,
Judith, Sarah and Esther. Jewish heroines.

Paul NYAGA,
Moral Consistency with Lonergan's Thought.

François FAURE,
Emmanuel Mounier : La personne est son engagement (T. 1).

François FAURE,
Emmanuel Mounier : Montrer, sans démontrer (T. 2).

Olivier-Thomas VENARD, Gregory TATUM,
Conversations sur Paul. « Supportez-vous les uns les autres ».

Isaac MUTELO,
Muslim Organisations in South Africa. Political Role Post-1948.

Stephen Musisi KASOZI,
Issues of Constitutionalism. A case study of Uganda.

Pierre Dalin DOMERSON,
La gestion des biens de l'Église. Enjeu Pastoral.

Philippe ANDRÈS,
Notre-Dame de Rocamadour. Du Moyen Âge à nos jours.

Oliver BARRETT,
Ecological Crisis. In Catholic Social Teaching.

Augustin WILIWOLI SIBILONI,
Négociation pacifique des conflits sociaux.

Alfred DIBAN KI,
Ubuntu et vie chrétienne.

Claude VALENTIN,
99 Questions sur l'Humanitaire.

Philippe MONTOISY,
Le chien militaire et la Première Guerre mondiale.

Alice NEPVEU-BARRIEUX,
La marine dans l'Ancien Testament. Représentations et enjeux.

Marie MONNET,
En chemin.

Christophe-Marie, O.P. MOGHA NGAMANAPO MUDAKA,
Quelle crise d'éducation ? Des slogans segmentés à l'hyperconscience de la liberté holistique.

Caroline FERRER,
Saint Jérôme. La représentation dans la collection Fesch en Corse.

Munguci D. ETRIGA,
Kwasi Wiredu. Thoughts. Conference proceeding from Tangaza University.

Isaac MUTELO,
Human Rights in Southern Africa. Theory and Practice.

Marc MITRI,
  Le christ-médecin. La divinisation de l'homme comme guérison selon Grégoire de Nysse.

Manuel RIVERO,
  Progresser dans la vérité. Père Marie-Joseph Lagrange, dominicain.

Bruno CALLEBAUT,
  Les évangiles au carrefour des exégèses.

Michel VAN AERDE,
  Domuni, une aventure collective. 1998 – 2023.

Didier PETERS,
  La chaise et l'électron. Analyse de la pensée d'Alfred North Whitehead.

Augustin WILIWOLI,
  Justice sociale : Nouveaux enjeux.

Claude VALENTIN,
  De Lascaux à l'intelligence artificielle. Histoire de la culture.

Michel VAN AERDE,
  Domuni, una aventura colectiva. 1998 – 2023.

Michel VAN AERDE,
  Domuni, a collective adventure. 1998 – 2023.

www.ingramcontent.com/pod-product-compliance
Lightning Source LLC
Chambersburg PA
CBHW070844160426
43192CB00012B/2298